Crete

Early History and Culture of Crete people

Author

Ranchowwy Nicholson

Copyright Notice

Copyright © 2017 Global Print Digital
All Rights Reserved

First Printing: 2017.

ISBN: 978-1-912483-41-9

Publisher: Global Print Digital.
Arlington Row, Bibury, Cirencester GL7 5ND
Gloucester
United Kingdom.
Website: www.homeworkoffer.com

.

Table of Content

Introduction

Crete is the largest island in Greece and the second biggest (after Cyprus) of the East Mediterranean. It lies at the Southern Aegean Sea and at the crossroads of three continents Europe, Asia and Africa. Crete covers an area of 8.336 sq.kms. The length of the island is 260 km, but the shore-length is 1.046 km. The biggest width is 60 km while the smallest is 12 km. A high mountain range crosses the island from West to East, formed by three different groups of mountains.

To the West the White Mountains (2.453 m), in the middle the mountain of Idi (Psiloritis-2.456 m) and to the East the mountain of Dikti (2.148 m). These mountains gifted Crete with fertile plateaus like Lassithi, Omalos and Nida, caves like Diktaion and Idaion cave, and gorges like the famous Gorge of Samaria.

There are also quite a few valleys and small plains. The largest and most important plain is that of Messara located between Psiloritis and Asterousia mountains at the centre - south of the island

History of Crete

Outlined history of the island of Crete, from Neolithic times to present days.

Neolithic Period (6500 - 2600 B.C)

No remains from the preneolithic period nave been found on Crete.

Before the Neolithic period, people must have lived in caves at first and supported themselves by hunting and fishing, using stone and bone tools, and they must have known how to make simple clay pots.

Later they seem to have developed a primitive agriculture and started to make clay houses on rock foundations, to tame animals and to decorate their pottery with different colors and patterns as well as making clay images of animals. The various finds made and the location of the first dwelling places lead to the supposition that this primitive civilization was not native and unique but part of the common eastern Mediterranean civilization.

Prepalatial (Early Minoan I, Ii, Iii) Period (2600 - 2000 B.C.)

During the last stages of the Neolithic period (up to about 2600 BC) this highly developed civilization reached its distinctive peak, known as the Minion Era. The people were short- the average male height was about 1.60 m. Nothing is known about commerceduring the period but it is assumed that there was trade with the nearby islands and the east.

Pottery making flourished and copper and later bronze began to be worked. A distinctive artistic sensitivity can be recognized in the seals of that period, worked in semiprecious stones. Revising Evans, archeologists call this period until 2000 BC the Prepalatial.

Protopalatial (Middle Minoan I, Ii, Iiia) Period(2000 - 1700 B.C)

The period from 2000 BC to 1700 BC is called the Protopalatial, with the construction of the first palaces at Knossos, Phaestos and Malia, as a result of the concentration of wealth and power in the hands of the ruling families in these settlements.

Following the development of productivity, an organized and hierarchic society had already come into being, with a corresponding decline in the clan system. Increasing trade with the other Aegean islands, Egypt and the rest of Africa, Asia Minor and the entire Mediterranean led to the emergence of Crete as a sea power. The import, processing and re-export of metal, together with intermediate trade, amassed wealth for the island. Writing was used, in the form of hieroglyphics, probably originating from Egypt. Work in gold and precious stones, sculpture and pottery reached amazing heights.

The palaces were destroyed, apparently by earthquakes, in 1700 BC but this did not interrupt the development of civilization, however. At about this time, a new form of writing, known as Linear A, made its appearance; it was probably used to record commercial and administrative matters. It has still not been decided whether the roots of this writing were Indo-European or Semitic.

Neopalatial (Middle Minoan Iiib - Late Minoan I, Ii) Period(1700 - 1400 B.C)

In the so-called Neopalatial period (1700 BC -1400 BC) the palaces at Knossos, Phaestos and Malia were rebuilt on a much grander scale; they were advanced even judged by modern standards. The bulk of Minoan power was centered undoubtedly around Knossos, but the other sites in central and eastern Crete show evidence of the wealth and activity of the Minoans. Minoan society resembled a pyramid, with the farmers and workers at the base and the legendary Minos at the top. The common people knew nothing of the luxurious and comfortable life of the palaces. Although this was not a matriarchal society, women had a privileged place and some of them must have had considerable influence at the palace.

The Mother-Goddess, source of Life and fertility occupied first place in religion. Her symbols were the double axe, horns, birds, snakes and flowers, all of which can be seen in the large frescoes which adorn the palace, as well as on the pottery. The art of this period reaches the peak of incomparable delicacy.

During this period Crete took part in international trade and there is proof that amber was imported from the Baltic along the "amber route", across Europe. Their wealth and power gave the Minoans the confidence to build their palaces proudly, without the protection of fortifications.

By about 1500 BC a new form of writing, called Linear B, had come into use; archaeologists have recognized it as Greek, which shows that there was a connection between the inhabitants of mainland Greece, the Achaeans (Mycenaeans) and those of Crete.

Postpalatial (Late Minoan Iii) Period (1400 - 1100 B.C)

In about 1450 BC a terrible disaster laid waste all the centers of Minoan Crete.

Was it earthquake again or revolution or were the places burnt by invaders?

What is certain, however, is that new rulers were appearing in the Aegean at that time.

The last flowering of Minoan art, known as "Postpalatial style", ended with the conquest of the island by the Achaeans. Not only did the typical Minoan characteristics vanish from society, art and religion, but Minoan grace and delicacy also disappeared from the arts and crafts of the period, which became rough and clumsy.

Knossos, Tylissos, Agia Triada and Palekastro were partly rebuilt and inhabited, while Minoans settled in new villages in eastern Crete at the same time.

The part played by the island in commerce, and its influence in general, was limited from then on, but Crete did take part in the Trojan War with its own army.

The Bronze Age and its world came to an end. Wars, social struggles, financial exhaustion all paved the way for the Dorian invasion.

Sub-Minoan Period (1100 - 1000 B.C)

In about 1100 BC the Dorians - a Greek race -captured the Minoan strongholds one after the other and put an end to the Mycenaean state. Crete then came under the sway of the new rulers and so ended the last Minoan period - the Postpalatial (1400 BC to 1100 BC).

With the occupation of Crete by the Dorians armed with iron weapons, the local population was reduced to slave status. Part of the population (called Eteocretans by the Greeks) sought refuge on the plateau of Lassithi and in the extreme east of Crete where they kept up the heritage of the Minoan language until the Hellenistic period.

Dorian Period (100 - 67 B.C)

Crete then passed into complete obscurity and the only work continued was the production of great earthenware jars (pithoi). Iron slowly took the place of bronze and in this new period it was the Phoenecians who dominated the Mediterranean. Crete re-established contact with the surrounding areas and started a new life, especially in the west of the island.

Phoenecian, Assyrian and Egyptian influence led to the substitution of the eastern style for the geometric. Crete was now just one part of the then known world and showed no sign of any particular culture of its own. The basis of the social structure of the time was land ownership. The aristocracy of great landowners formed the ruling class of the Dorians who had civil rights and lived under a socialist regime.

The great families of clans came to power in turn every year and they were represented by ten noblemen who had civil, military, religious and judicial duties. Former representatives formed a senate whose power in important matters was unlimited even by the assembly of citizens. Young men underwent military training in "herds" before taking an oath. They were then grouped in companies and had their meals at common mess tables, at public expense.The citizens were free but were obliged to enlist in the army. The farmers were divided into Perioikioi (neighbours) and serfs, according to birth.

The Dorians on Crete were especially advanced in matters of legislation, as is shown by the laws found at Gortys. Thanks to trade, there was still some degree of prosperity on the island, which enabled the Cretan cities, already formed into independent city-states, to construct beautiful buildings and issue their own coinage. Knossos, Gortys and Kydonia ruled over the smaller settlements.

In about 300 BC six of the south-western cities formed the "Highland Confederation" which later formed alliances with Gortys, Cyrenaica and Pergamos. Other Cretan cities made alliances with other powers, such as

Sparta and Rhodes, but these alliances were never long lasting.

Endless skirmishes, raids and wars brought the island into disrepute and at this time Crete was known as a refuge for pirates, beggars and liars. There was now no stopping the fall of Crete.

Roman Period (67 B.C. - 395 A.D.)

The Romans arrived in Crete as mediators and settled in as conquerors. After three years' sporadic fighting, Crete became a Roman province, with Gortys as the capital of both Crete and Cyrenaica. Under Roman rule, which brought peace and some autonomy to the island, Crete enjoyed a period of prosperity, as the many Roman remains show.

First Byzantine Period (395 - 824 A.D.)

Titus, the first Bishop of Gortys. converted the population to Christianity, by order of the Apostle Paul, according to tradition. After the division of Roman

Empire into western and eastern sectors, Crete came under the Byzantine sphere of influence.

During this period Christianity spread and many churches were built on Crete. One of the biggest is Ayios Titus at Gortys (AD 600). From the political and cultural point of view, however, Crete is lacking in interest during this time.

Arab Occupation (824- 961 A.D.)

From AD 824 to 961 Crete was occupied by the Arabs. The center of the island was the fort of Rabd el Khandak, which later became known as Handax Or Candia and which is now the city of Heraklion. Apart from coins, no remains have been found from this period. After a struggle lasting for many years, Nikiforos Fokas finally succeeded in freeing Crete from the Arabs and the second Byzantine Period lasted from AD 961 -AD 1204.

Second Byzantine Period (961 - 1204 A.D.)

Noble families from Byzantium, merchants from Europe and Christians from eastern countries settled in Crete. Attempts were made to destroy all traces of the Arabs and to bring back to Christianity all those who had become Moslems. Crete became of some significance again. When Byzantium became a victim of the 4th Crusade, Crete was granted to Boniface II, Count of Momferato, who then sold it to the Venetians.

Before they could take possession, however, the Genoese under Erico Pescatori seized the island. They built 14 forts around the island and fought the Venetian fleet for four years before finally yielding in 1210.

Venetian Occupation (1204 - 1669 A.D.)

The Venetian occupation lasted for 450 years. Crete was divided into fiefs (feudal territories), which were handed over to Venetian colonists and entrepreneurs.

They named the island and the capital city "Candia" from the Arab name for the city; they organized and fortified and gave Crete a new brilliance. The surviving Venetian fortifications and castles remain in good condition today. During the first half of the Venetian occupation there were many bloody uprisings against the cruel overlords and their efforts to impose their alien way of life and to convert the Cretan population from Orthodox Christianity to Roman Catholicism - starting from the top with the Archbishop and Bishops.

Even the Venetians took part in the 1363 rebellion against the imposition of taxes and the privileges demanded by Venice. Sometimes these uprisings were crushed and bloody reprisals taken and at other times they ended in compromise with concessions being made to the rebels.

Many artists and scholars had found refuge in Crete during the decline of the Byzantine Empire and after the fall of Byzantium itself. They established schools and Orthodox monasteries and literature and art flourished. Despite the Venetian influence, Cretan traditions continued.

Turkish Occupation (1669 - 1898 A.D.)

The Turkish attempt to conquer the island started with a pirate raid against the coastal towns and in 1645 the Turks captured Chania and then Rethymnon a year later, in spite of Venetian resistance.

The siege and heroic defense of Candia (Heraklion) began in 1648 and was to last for 22 years. With bated breath, Europe watched the longest siege in history. It was the last stronghold of Christianity in the area and the Pope made a general appeal for help for the beleaguered city. Francesco Morosini led the defense of the island but had to surrender eventually.

The Turks allowed the defenders to leave with honor and almost the entire Cretan population deserted the city, together with the foreigners. The Cretans left their island and settled on the Ionian islands and in Venice and Mani. From Mani, some went on to Corsica, where a form of the Cretan dialect can still be heard today. History relates that during the battle for Heraklion the Venetians and their allies lost 31.000 men and the Turks lost 118.000.

Crete was then shared out among the pashas, with the exception of Sfakia which, although it paid a symbolic tax to the Turks, remained independent and became a refuge for insurgents and persecuted Cretans. Although relatively few Turks settled on the island, a great many Christians were forced to become Moslem in order to survive and many more had to leave the cities for the mountains. This was a result of declining agriculture and trade caused by the weak administrative organization of the Turks and of the ever-increasing taxes and tarrifs arbitrarily imposed on the local population.

Under these inhuman conditions, nobody had any inclination to work and this in turn made the terrible position of the local inhabitants even worse, while earthquakes and uprisings destroyed the villages. The first great uprising took place in 1770, led by the Sfakian, Daskalogiannis. When the Greek Revolution started in 1821 , Crete rose too but was shameful abandoned by the Great Powers and ceded to the Egyptians, who had been called in by the Turks to help them. The Turks took over again in 1840, but the Cretans did not give up and the revolution continued, with its unsparing outpouring of blood. The years 1866-69 stand out particularly, as does the typical, stirring example of the holocaust of Arkadi.

Semi Autonomy - Union with Greece (1989 - 1941 A.D.)

The Great Powers finally intervened in 1898 and Crete became independent under their guarantee; with a High Commissioner, Prince George, younger son of the

King of Greece. In 1905 the Cretans rose again, led by Eleftherios Venizelos, this time because they wanted union with Greece. Prince George was compelled to resign. Union finally came in 1913 and so together Crete and Greece faced the consequences of World War I and the catastrophe of Asia Minor.

German Occupation (1941 - 1945 A.D.)

No sooner had the island begun to recover and even to prosper, than World War II began. In 1941 select German paratroopers invaded Crete from the air; during the Battle of Crete the Cretans, both men and women, fought magnificently and inflicted extremely heavy casualties on the Germans. For four years Crete was occupied once again, but the island fought on in spite of forced labour, starvation, inhuman cruelty, the burning of entire villages and the execution of thousands of Cretans. One impressive page of the Cretan resistance was written when General Kreipe was kidnapped. The last Germans left Crete in July 1945 and the long-suffering island was free again.

Post War (1945 A.D. - Today

Crete avoids worst of Greek civil war. Economic development and exploitation of touristic and archaeological resources hit full stride.

Heraklion Town

Heraklion Environment

Heraklion is the largest city in Crete (and fifth in Greece) with a population in excess of 120000. It concentrates most of the economic activity of the island, and is the main port of entry to Crete for the majority of visitors and commodities.

Iraklion (GR: Ηράκλειον - also transliterated as Heraklion or Herakleion) is the largest urban centre in Crete, the capital of the region and the economic centre of the island. The first European civilisation, the Minoan civilisation, flourished on this land 5000 years ago. Currently the population of the municipality of

Heraklion is approximately 150.000 people. It is a very dynamic and cosmopolitan town, particularly during the summer period when thousands of visitors can be seen shopping in the market or visiting the museums and other places of interest. During the last 20 years the city has made also a remarkable progress in the academic and technological fields.

Heraklion lies along the North coast of the island, having to the west at about 80 km the town of Rethymnon and at 135 km the city of Hania. To the east is the town of Agios Nikolaos (60km) and the town of Sitia (130km)

Access

The Heraklion airport (HER), named after the Cretan writer Nikos Kazantzakis, is one of the biggest in Greece and receives approximately 15% of the total tourist traffic of Greece. Heraklion's airport is about 5km east of the city. Major car-rental companies have desks at the airport. Taxi and public bus are available for transfer from/to Iraklion.

Iraklion also receives a lot of visitors by boat. There are daily ferry trips to and from Peiraeus (Athens' port), and many weekly ones to and from other islands and towns in Greece. The terminal at Heraklion port is within walking distance from the town's center and there is plenty of taxis to take visitors to their destinations.

The Crete intra regional Bus terminal is also located close to the port.

Facilities to visitors

Heraklion today, as a modern town, has extensive facilities that cater for all needs of its visitors. There is a lot of hotels ranging from Luxury class to small rent-a-room and youth hostels operating all year round. Most of them are located in the old town.

Travel bureaus offering excursions and special events, car hire companies and other tourist related agencies are also close to the old town's center and the port.

As far as entertainment goes the options are almost unlimited. Herakliotes are a people that enjoy going out a lot, either for lunch, dinner, a coffee or a drink, or all of them - the weather, of course, helps a lot to this. So there is plenty of restaurants, family taverns, luxury café - snack bars, traditional coffee shops (Kafeneia), music halls with traditional Cretan or Bouzouki (Rebetica songs), discos, small pubs and music bars, either indoors or outdoors, open throughout the year and frequented by visitors and locals alike.

Heraklion, being the business center of the area, has plenty of stores selling clothes, shoes, jewelery etc. Stores are open in the morning (9 a.m. to 2 p.m.) and in the evening (5 p.m. to 9 p.m.) with the exception of the evenings of Monday, Wednesday and Saturday.

Cultural Life

Heraklion's long history and cosmopolitan character is reflected to its rich cultural life throughout the year. A wealth of cultural events from music & dance recitals to theatrical performances, to lectures, to art exhibitions and much more are hosted in the many private or public places that the city offers.

The major cultural event in Heraklion is the summer cultural festival, organised by the municipality. It is a three-month extravaganza of music, theatre and dance, both of Greek and foreign performers. Most concerts take place outdoors at several outdoor theatres which have been created out of the bastions of the Venetian walls, adding to the scenery of every performance.

The Heraklion's carnival celebration and parade, the municipal cinema and the Mediterranean Festival of

Arts (25 September-05 October) are organised also by the municipality of Heraklion

Sightseeing

History is very much alive in the old town of Heraklion, just like in most Greek cities.

From the old Venetian Harbour, the August 25th Str., leads to the old town's centre. The central square while surrounded by cafes, stores and restaurants, is dominated by the fountain of the Lions, built by Morozini the venetian governor in 1628. The Town Hall, is today housed in the Venetian Loggia, a building from the same era and next to it, the plateau and the cathedral of Agios Titos an exceptional monument from the Byzantine era.

From the central square the street of the "Central Market" ends at "Kornarou Square" with the coffee house, housed at "Koubes" a Turkish fountain and next to it the "Bembo fountain" built by a Venetian nobleman. To the left "Averof Str." leads to "Eleftherias sq." , Heraklion's main square where the Archaeological museum stands and to the right 'Kyrillou Loukareos Str" leads to Agios Minas cathedral and Agia Aikaterini Museum.

All around the old part of the city, a visitor can walk following the Venetian walls that meet at the old port and "Koules", the fortress that dominates the old harbour of the city.

The visitor to Heraklion should definitely visit the archaeological site at Knossos and the Archaelogical Museum of Heraklion that houses most of the Minoan findings in Crete. Special attention should also be paid to the Historical museum of Heraklion that houses findings from the early Christian era to today and the Museum of Natural History

History

To date no Minoan remains have been uncovered within the boundaries of ancient or medieval Heraklion. Nevertheless, the harbour town serving Knossos stood for approximately 2000 years on the site of the modern port and the eastern suburbs of Poros and Katsambas.

Large houses, major workshop facilities and sumptuous rock-cut cave and tholos tombs have been located at the estuary of the River Kairatos, which flows down from Knossos. Excavations have unearthed a significant portion of the town and several dozen tombs. The recent discovery of boathouses in the harbour town by the mouth of the Kairatos at Katsambas is of major significance.

From post-Minoan to Roman times (900 B.C. - 330)
According to historical sources, in post-Minoan times a small town named Herakleion, which may have served as a harbour for Knossos, stood on the site of the

present city. This was located in the area around and to the west of the Archaeological Museum.

The Name "Heraklion" was first used during the 1821 revolution. Its existence as a place name had of course been known since antiquity, and was chosen by the revolutionaries to boost national consciousness and link the revolutionary present to the glorious past. Over the following decades the name was used with increasing frequency by Greek intellectuals, merchants and several locals, until it acquired the official sanction of the Ottoman authorities in the Organic Act of 1869.

In parallel with the new name, ordinary folk did of course continue to use earlier names for the town: Megalo Kastro, Kastro and Chora (the last being a generic term used for Greek island capitals).

From the late 6th century onwards the earlier urban centres fell into decline and the population moved into the countryside. The Arabs had control of the trade routes to the East, and external trade began to wane.

From the 7th century onwards the island was subject to repeated pirate raids, led mainly by the Arabs, which brought about the decline of coastal settlements. The inhabitants moved inland to small farming settlements. To deal with this new threat Crete was upgraded to a theme, with Gortyn remaining the administrative, ecclesiastical and economic centre.

In this period there was a settlement identified as Roman Herakleion, which came within the jurisdiction of the Diocese of Knossos. Theodoros, Bishop of Herakleioupolis, is referred to in the Proceedings of the VI Oecumenical Council (786-7) as being third in the hierarchy of the eleven bishops of Crete. By this time Kastro may well have been in use as a place name for the settlement.

Heraklion was build by the Arab Saracens in 824 A.D.. At the time it was called Chandax, a name adapted from the Arab word "kandak" that means moat , due to the moat that the Saracens dug all around the city. Iraklion was built on the location where the old harbour of Knossos used to stand. The name survived during the second Byzantine period as Chandakas, and during the Venetian occupation as Candia. In fact during the Venetian occupation , the whole island was named Candia after the city.

The Saracens occupation lasted 140 years (824 -961 A.D). During that time Chandax was the safe harbour of the pirates that ravaged and looted the eastern Mediterranean.Immeasurable wealth was concentrated in Chandax, loot from the islands sacked and ships sunk by the pirates.

The Byzantines tried quite a few times to liberate Chandax, with Nikiforos Fokas finally succeeding in 961

A.D. After a long and bloody siege that lasted almost a year. The fort and the walls surrouding the city were totally demolished, and the city burned down. Most of the Saracens were slaughtered, with the rest of them taken prisoners to Konstantinoupolis.

All the valuable possesions of the Saracens were taken also to Konstantinoupolis. According to the historians of the era it took 300 ships to move all that to the capital of Byzantium.Some of these treasures survided through the ages and are on display on the monastery of Megistis Layras at mount Athos.

The sack of Chandax by the Byzantines, marks the beginning of the second Byzantine era which lasted until 1204.

At that time Alexios the 4th heir to the emperor of Byzantium Isaakios the 2nd, who was dethroned by his brother Alexios the 3rd, asked the Pope to help him get back his throne.He was referred to the Crusaders who at the time were starting the Fourth Crusade, and agreed to give Crete to them once they reestablished him to the throne of Byzantium.

Eventually , the Venetians were established in Chandax in 1210. They rebuilted the walls of the fort in order to protect themselves from the rebellions of the locals, the most important being that of the Kallergis in 1367.

Although the Venetians were hated by the locals , and the whole of the island suffered under their yoke, Chandax became probably the most important cultural center in the East Mediterranean during the Renaissance. Many Cretans studied in the island and abroad in Italy, and became famous (the painter El Greco , Dominicos Theotokopoulos, who was born in Fodele - Iraklion being the best known) .Chandax was a shining light that kept Hellenism alive during these dark times.

After the crashing of the revolution in 1367 the danger from the Cretans had passed. But a new enemy was rising across the sea, the Turks. So in 1462 the rulers of the city decided to rebuilt and strengthen the walls again. The new wall was designed by one of the most famous military engineers of Venice, Michele Sammicheli. The construction lasted 100 years. This huge project was funded by extra taxation of the Cretan people, and carried out by the locals who were practically conscripted to work on it. Every Cretan from 14 to 60 years old was forced to work a week every year on the construction.

These walls are tremendous. At some points they are 60 meters thick.

There perimeter is 5.5 km and there are 12 bastions and forts all around. The best known is the Martinengo Bastion, were currently the grave of the great Greek writer Nikos Kazantzakis is located.

And yet, for all there size and splendour, these walls fell .

The Turks managed to occupy Chandax in 1669 , after a siege that lasted 22 years!!. But the cost in human life was appaling. After these 22 years 30.000 Christians were dead and 120.000 Turks.

The Turks occupied Crete untill 1897. During that time numerous rebellions by the Cretans were crashed. On August 25 ,1897 Cretans were slaughtered on the main road to the harbour from the city.

This road is still named after the event , 25th of August Street. After that, and following negotiations with the Ottomans, Crete was granted autonomy. During these negotiations, the political star of a great statesman appeared that influenced politics not only for Crete and Greece, but for the whole of Balcans, Eleftherios Venizelos.

Crete was an independent state from 1897 to 1913. During that time the longing of the Cretans to unite with their brothers in Greece remained. Venizelos became the Prime Minister of Greece in 1909 and continued his efforts to unite Crete with Greece. Eventually , and as a result of the Balkan wars of 1912-13, he succeeded.

From then on the island was an integral part of the Greek state, with its own share in the political and military misadventures of the ensuing years. The Asia Minor disaster in 1922 dealt the final blow to the "Megali Idea", while also marking the beginning of the Greek interwar period (1922-1940). The Greek state then set its sights on internal reorganization and the rehabilitation of over a million refugees.

Thousands of refugees settled on Crete, particularly in Heraklion. At the same time, the last 23 821 Muslim residents were forced to abandon the island. The population grew apace, as new suburbs such as Nea Alikarnassos, Tria Pefka, Katsambas and Patelles were added to the townscape.

Marked changes in the inhabitants' everyday life also occurred. The port was extended, the number of cars on the streets multiplied and the town acquired an aerodrome. Concrete, electricity, the telephone and the radio appeared on the scene in Heraklion, altering time-worn habits and practices. On the eve of World War II, Heraklion was by sight a booming modern urban centre, with bustling mercantile and shipping activity and a lively social scene.

The Italian offensive launched against Greece on 28th October 1940 brought an end to the twenty-year Greek inter-war period, forcing the country to become embroiled in global conflict. Together with Greek victories, the failure of the Italian attack at a time when the Axis powers appeared invincible was hailed with great enthusiasm in democratic countries, yet at the same time provoked German intervention. On 6th April 1941, the German army invaded Greece via the Bulgarian-Greek border, just when the main bulk of the Greek army was fighting on the Albanian front. Despite desperate resistance put up by Greek and British forces, the front collapsed, and by late April almost all Greek territory was under occupation. Crete's hour had come.

Parachute drop during the Battle of Crete, 1940 At 17:30 in the afternoon of 20th May 1941, the sky above Heraklion filled with Junkers Ju52 transport planes, bearing the men of the 1st Parachute Regiment under the command of Colonel Bruno Oswald Bräuer. Codenamed Orion, this force's mission was to take the city and the aerodrome. The reception accorded by the defenders was "extremely warm", with several aeroplanes being hit before the paratroopers could even jump. Fighting on the ground was intense, as dozens of people from the town and surrounding villages flocked to help in fighting off the invasion. Particularly in the area around the aerodrome, the attackers were pinned down from the very first moment.

The following morning, divisions of paratroopers capitalizing on a renewed aerial bombardment succeeded in getting inside the walls, mainly via the Chania Gate. Street battles broke out in the town, leading to heavy losses on both sides. Finally, in the course of the night, the defenders managed to clear the town and suburbs as far as Tsalikaki and Estavromenos. On the following day Heraklion suffered violent aerial bombardment, aimed at relieving the sorely tried paratroop forces.

Clashes continued over the ensuing days, but the taking of Maleme aerodrome rendered any further defence futile. At daybreak on the 29th of the month, the last British soldiers boarded the warships that had reached Heraklion harbour. At noon on the same day, the town fell to German forces.

Over the course of time, the first resistance groups were set up, aimed at reconnaissance, acts of sabotage and the formation of guerrilla groups. The resistance movement mushroomed day by day. Battles between the occupying forces and guerrillas, sabotage attacks on German installations, executions of collaborators and other high-risk activities became a part of the new reality.

From September 1944 onwards, German and Italian forces began withdrawing from the island's eastern sectors. In Heraklion, the long-awaited day of liberation dawned on 11th October. The atmosphere in the town was highly charged as the last of the Germans withdrew to the jeers of the assembled crowds and the guerrillas, who then entered. Nevertheless, the moment the German rearguard passed through the Chania Gate and further on out, accompanied by Allied officers, the crowds broke out into cheers and songs.

German troops from all corners of the island gathered in the area around the town of Chania. Allied forces and guerrillas avoided attacking them so as not to cause any further damage to the troubled island. There they remained in fortified positions until the final German surrender on 8th May 1945.

Sightseeing

Archaeological Museum of Herakleion

History

The Museum collections began being put together in the late 19th century, when Crete was still under Ottoman rule. In 1878, during a period of temporary calm following the insurrection of the Cretan people, when the Turkish government granted certain freedoms and Crete was acknowledged as A privileged and autonomous province of the Ottoman state, a group of distinguished citizens established the Educational Association of Herakleion with a view to founding schools and developing Greek education and culture on the island.

In 1883 under its new chairman, the antiquity-loving doctor Joseph Hadzidakis, the Association expanded its activities and having secured a special written decree from the Sultan, obtained recognition as a quasi - official archaeological authority and devoted itself to collecting Cretan antiquities with a view to establishing a Cretan Museum. Donations of local private collections were gradually added to the artefacts gathered by the Association. This important archaeological material was originally housed in two rooms in the churchyard of the Cathedral of Aghios Minas and in this way was saved thanks to the actions of Hadzidakis, during the turmoil of the 1896 uprising. In 1899 the struggles of the Cretan people for freedom were vindicated. And the autonomy of Crete was recognised under the protection of the four Great Powers. The Association ceded the Cretan Museum to the Cretan Polity, and an archaeological law was passed immediately by which two archaeological districts were designated under ephors Ioseph Hadzidaikis and Stephanos Xanthoudidis.

In 1900 with the proclamation of the autonomy of Crete, the Museum's significant acquisitions were housed in part of a barracks building, which today accommodates the Prefecture of Iraklion. At the same time intense excavation activity had been undertaken by the Greek ephors and by foreign scholars and archaeological schools who showed a lively interest in Cretan antiquities. The growing number of splendid finds required the construction of a special building to accommodate them.

Thus between 1904 and 1907 a large open - plan museum was built and one year later, a rear porch (opisthodomos) was added. In conformity with the general plan of a Classicist order drawn up by Panagiotis Kavvadias and the famous architect - archaeologist Wilhelm Dorpfeld, the west wing and the Classical - style facade were added in 1912. Nevertheless this building, from the point of view of space, functionality and quality of construction was, from the outset, totally inadequate to provide secure housing and exhibition space for the Museum's unique archaeological treasure, which kept growing with the addition of important finds from excavations.

Immediately after construction of the Museum and especially after 1913 - 1914 when Crete became part of Greece, the demand was put forward to construct a more suitable, modern Museum. After Hadzidakis' retirement in 1923 and Xanthoudidis untimely death in 1928 the issue was raised again by the next active ephor Spyros Marinatos. In the meantime, the building had suffered further serious fatigue after successive earthquakes. In I934, work began on the new building in which the Museum is housed to this day. Between 1937 and the outbreak of World War II, it was virtually completed

It was built on the same prominent site as the previous building, which was demolished, at a central location in the city of Herakleion, on the inner side of the eastern Venetian wall near the ruins of the famous Venetian church of Aghios Frankiskos. The anti - seismic building, with a total area of 8.800 sq.m, built to a design drawn up in 1933 by architect Patroklos Karantinos (1903 - 1976), is one of the most significant products of the modem architectural movement in Greece during the interwar period. It is an avant-garde building in terms of both style and functionality, with applications that were innovative for their time on a global scale, such as the special lighting system with the use of light wells.

It is regarded as one of the most important international works of the "new architecture". A characteristic fact is that, in a significant early post - war catalogue, it was assessed as being one of the eight most representative European "exhibition and recreation buildings" among museums in Italy, Finland, Spain and Austria. Even though it is not particularly well known and despite the fact that the 1933 design was not applied in full, the Herakleion Museum building constitutes a top-ranking example of 20th – century Greek architecture and a point of reference for significant works by other important architects, such as the National Gallery in Athens, the Museum in Ioannina, etc.

The re - exhibition of the ancient artefacts began in 1951, overseen by the then ephor Nikolaos Platon; at the same time new storage facilities were built. In 1952 the main exhibition had already been presented. In

1964, the next ephor, Stylianos Alexiou designed a new wing that included four additional halls.

The Museum today comprises twenty halls that are open to the public, the Scholarly Collection that is open to researchers and scholars alone and also contains significant finds, storage areas and conservation workshops. Exhibits from the Neolithic, Minoan. Geometric and Archaic periods and sculptures from the Hellenic and Roman periods can be found on the ground floor. On the upper floor are the Minoan wall paintings and, since 2002, the exhibition entitled "The King Minos" featuring gold Minoan signet and other rings.

The Archaic. Hellenistic and Roman small artefacts and the Giamalakis Collection, which were once displayed in two halls on the upper floor, have been withdrawn, owing to the many travelling exhibitions.

Despite the extreme importance of its works from the Hellenic period, the singularity of the Museum lies in the wealth of Minoan masterpieces that constitute its primary exhibition material.

The more than 10.000 artefacts found in Minoan palaces, villas, settlements, shrines and cemeteries illustrate the panorama of the Minoan world and demonstrate its amazing diversity. Among them, emblematic and celebrated works can be singled out, such as the snake goddesses, the bull's head rhyton, the Prince with the Lilies, the bull-leaping fresco, the gold bees, the "Parisienne", the Harvesters' Vase and many others.

It is obvious that, as almost fifty years have elapsed since the last reorganisation, the Museum was urgently in need of radical renovation, as regards both the building and the exhibition. The remodelling of the building includes extensions, additions and modern infrastructure works and is already taking place on the basis of plans drawn up by architect Alexandros Tombazis. This will be followed by the re-exhibition of old collections and new finds, structured into chronological and thematic units in accordance with modern museological specifications, so that the significance, development and continuity of the ancient Cretan civilisation over a period of seven millennia, from the 7th millennium BC to the 4th century AD, can be displayed with emphasis on the singularity of the Minoan collection.

Knossos

The celebrated palace of Knossos, the most magnificent Minoan monument, residence of the mythical king Minos, was for about three hundred years - from 1650 BC to 1350 BC - the main centre of power in Crete. Its history is even longer and its architecture as complex as its functions. The palace was built early in the second millennium and destroyed two hundred years later, at the end of the Palaeopalatial period. It was rebuilt in a more splendid form, suffered fresh disasters and repairs and was ultimately destroyed by fire in 1350 BC. For the last hundred years of its life, it was the seat of the Mycenaean dynasty that had succeeded the Minoan kings after the large scale disaster in Crete in 1450 BC and the collapse of the Minoan palace system.

Built with sumptuous materials, on the basis of an intricate and coherent architectural design, using highly advanced construction techniques, and boasting an impressive water supply and sewage system, the palace of Knossos, twice the size (ca. 22.000 sq. meters and 1.400 rooms) of the other two large palaces at Phaistos and Malia, is the monumental symbol of the Minoan civilisation. Labyrinthine corridors and the famous Grand Staircase linked the multiple areas of buildings from three to five storeys high that were situated around the Central Court.

The west wing housed the religious and cult activities; in the east wing were the royal apartments. The palace contained large storerooms in which were enormous storage jars (pitharia) and various workshops. The South Propylaeum and North Entrance were fortified by colonnaded bastions. Public events were held in the so-called Theatre with the Royal Road and the open-air Courts. The Throne Room, with its wall paintings and contiguous underground purification tank (or "Lustral Basin'), was the most official venue for religious activities. This was where the famous "Throne of Minos' was located. the alabaster throne on which - according to Arthur Evans, the archaeologist who excavated Knossos - sat the "King - Priest', the secular and religious leader, and head of the senior officials who were seated on the benches surrounding the throne.

Many of the exceptional exhibits in the Herakleion Museum have come from the excavation of the palace and the large structures around it, including some of its most famous works, symbols of Minoan civilisation, such as the Snake Goddesses and other findings from the Sacred Treasuries, the rhyton in the shape of a bull`s head, the ivory bull - leaper, the relief wall painting of the "Prince with the Lilies', the wall painting of the bull - leaping, and others.

The architecture of the Minoan palaces was magnificent. At first glance, it seems that improvisation was the order of the day and that one area joins another, seemingly haphazardly, that everything is arranged simply around a central court and that all the structures rise from different levels. This is what the casual observer sees, but a closer look is enough to reveal the existence of a coherent plan. The ingenious design and the perfect organization of space enabled the builders to find a wonderful solution to the problems of light, air and drainage in the great palaces

-problems which still present difficulties even today.

Monuments

West court - West facade

Knossos Palace

The court is crossed by the so-called "Processional Causeways", which stand out from the rest of the paving and intersect each other. One idea is that processions paraded along them during ceremonies.

The West Facade of the Palace rises up along one side. The facade is constructed of massive gypsum blocks (orthostats) set on a plinth. The facade is indented or protrudes corresponding to the interior arrangement of space.

In front of the West Façade, two bases can be seen, thought to belong to stone-built altars. Settlement remains of the Neolithic (6700 - 3200 B.C.) and prepalatial (3200 - 1900 B.C.) periods have been found beneath the level of the "West Court".

Kouloures

Knossos Palace

Three large pits, known as "kouloures" (rings), with stone-lined walls were built in the West Court during the Old Palace period (1900-1700B.C.). The excavation workmen gave them their name and A. Evans kept it. The function of the circular pits is not clear. They have been interpreted as rubbish dumps either for all the refuse from the Palace or just the left-overs from sacred offerings. Support has also been given to the idea that they were storing grain.

In two of them, it is possible to see the remains of houses of the Pre Palatial period (3200-1900 B.C.). In the New Palace period (1700-1450 B.C.),the "kouloures" were covered over and out of use.

West Porch

Knossos Palace

The "West Porch" was a roofed area opening onto the Court, supported by one column of which part of the gypsum base remains. The east wall was decorated with a bull-leaping fresco. There was a small "guard-room" at the back.

The porch was closed off by a double door and from here began the long "Corridor of the Procession".

The Corridor of the Procession

Knossos Palace

The Corridor of the Procession is named from the wall painting decorating its east wall and depicting a procession of musicians and other people holding gifts. The floor was very fine. The "Corridor of the Procession", according to Evans, initially led to the "South Propylaeum" and continued on to the Central Court.

Today a causeway made of wood, with handrail, stands in its place, so the visitors can follow the same route.

The South Propylaeum

Knossos Palace

The "South Propylaeum", as we see it today, is a result of the restoration of Evans who put up a copy of the "Cup-Bearer" fresco here. The wall painting depicted a man holding a libation vase (rhyton). Its theme is connected with the "Procession Fresco" which, according to Evans, reached here, the "South Propylaeum". The pithoi (large storage jars) on the east side of the Propylaeum belong to the Postpalatial Period (1450-1100 B.C.), and indicate that the area was later used for storage.

The South Entrance

Knossos Palace

The south part and south facade of the palace is very eroded. Today one can only see foundations on tiered levels. At the bottom, a tower-like projection is all that remains of the south entrance to the Palace. An asceding corridor led to the Central Court.

The section of the corridor closest to the Central Court was reconstructed by Evans who put here a copy of a relief wall painting, of which only few fragments were found. On these fragments, it was possible to make out a figure wearing jewellery in the shape of lilies. The reconstruction we see here is uncertain. In Evans's opinion, it represented the "Priest-King". Other scholars think that it is a prince, whilst others believe it depicts a female figure. Anyway the original fresco which is known as the "Prince of Lilies" is one of the masterpieces in the collection of the Heraklion Museum.

West Magazines

Knossos Palace

North of the South Propylaeum, at a lower level there

is the start of the corridor that joins eighteen long and narrow storerooms, covering an area of 1300 sq.m.

In the floor of both the storerooms and corridor, there are ninety three rectangular cists, the so called "Kasellas". From the finds it appears they were used for keeping safe precious equipment and vases. There are also even larger cists in the corridor, internally lined, perhaps to hold liquids.

The pithoi (large storage jars) of the "West Magazines" bear witness to the wealth of the palace. The remains of some 150 pithoi were found, although there is room for about 400. Their contents are unknown, although they could have oil, wine, pulses, etc.

At different points of the magazine, clay tablets came to light in the Linear B script with records of an economic character. At the north end of the corridor, a large number of older clay seal impressions and clay tablets in the Cretan Hieroglyphic script were discovered.

The Throne Room

Knossos Palace

The antechamber of a complex of rooms that Evans named the "Throne Room".

Its name comes from the stone seat found in the room behind the antechamber, and between them were discovered traces of a burnt wooden construction. Today, a wooden seat has been placed here which is a copy of the stone one in the neighbouring chamber. After the antechamber is the central room of the complex. Right and left of the stone seat are yet more stone benches.

Pieces of fresco depicting plants and griffins, mythical beasts with a lion's body and bird's head were found in the same room. The restored fresco is in Heraklion Museum. Evans put a copy in its place. Stone vases for oil, often connected with rituals, were found on the floor. The stone basin you see was actually found in a neighbouring corridor and placed here. To the left, a low partition wall with a purification ceremonies and therefore called them "Lustral Basins".

The central room connects at the back with a series of small, dark rooms which were lit by lamps, as the finds illustrate.

The function of the complex is difficult to determine. Evans believed that the rooms were used for ceremonies with the main figure being the king of Knossos in his religious capacity. However, it seems unlikely to have been a Throne Room in the modern sense of the word.

The Tripartite Shrine

Knossos Palace

To the south of the Throne Room and the stairs, lies the area that has been identified as a shrine, called by Evans the "Tripartite Shrine" (Evans's restoration drawing). Its facade had columns and was divided into three parts, the central element being the highest.

There is a depiction of a comparable shrine on a wall painting now on display in Heraklion Museum. Inside the shrine were found clay tablets in the Linear B script and clay seal impressions which were possibly connected with the archive of a shrine.

The remaining areas behind the "Tripartite Shrine" are thought to have been connected with the sanctuaries of the palace. At the back, two small dark rooms with pillars are known as the "Pillar Crypts". The depresions in their floor are said to indicate that these rooms were used for libations. In another room, two large, rectangular, stone-built repositories were found, sunk into the floor. They were full of clay vases and valuable objects, amongst which were the statuettes representing the "Shake Goddess". The repositories have been interpreted as the "Temlple Repositories". The stairs on the right lead from the Central court to the upper floor of the West wing. This is largely reconstructed by Evans.

The Piano Nobile

Knossos Palace

The great staircase and the upper floor to which it leads are largely Evans' creation. Evans thought that it had a function rather like the first floor of Italian Palazzi of the Renaissance, which was called Piano Nobile. In this instance, he considered that the important reception rooms of the palace would lie on the upper floor. Evans also thought that there existed a shrine, the "Tri-Columnar Shrine", and its Treasury. The basis for his restoration lies in the column and pillar bases and the ritual stone vases found collapsed onto the ground floor, like the alabaster one in the shape of a lioness head. The rectangular building next to the stairs was built a long time after the destruction of the palace. Evans interpreted it as a "Greek Temple" based on finds of the historic period.

The Central Court

Knossos Palace

The Central Court (dimensions ca. 50m x 25 m.) is an architectural element common to all Minoan palaces. The Court connects the different wings with one another. There was also direct access from outside the Palace. Part of the paving, which once covered the whole court, is preserved in the northwest and southwest corners, whilst near the "Throne Room", parts of the drainage system can be made out which ensured the evacuation of rain water.

It is thought that the area must have been for meetings and rituals of both a sacred and profane character

The orientation of the Central Court was north-south with a clear view of the sacred Mount Giouhtas, where an important sanctuary was located.

East Wing - Grand Staircase

Knossos Palace

A large part of the east wing cannot be seen from the

Central Court as it is built into the side of the hill on top of which lies the rest of the Palace. It is one of the most interesting parts of the palace because two storeys are preserved below the level of the Central Court. Today, a large part of it has been reconstructed in concrete. The storeys are connected with one another by means of a system of stairs known as the "Grand Staircase". The staircase was found during the excavation in its original position. There is a total of four flights of stairs, two for each storey. The two lower flights are preserved as they were found. The steps are broad and deep, with a gentle incline that makes for an easy ascent. The staircase is lit by a large light-well and was surrounded by a colonnade of wooden columns.

The Grand Staircase

The Grand Staircase

The Grand Staircase & Hall of Colonades - First floor

The Grand Staircase & Hall of Colonades - Ground floor

A series of corridors, spacious halls and small rooms is

connected to the Grand Staircase. Evans, who believed that the Palace was the seat of the king of Knossos, hypnothesized that the residential quarters of the Royal family lay in this part of the site.

Shrine of the Double Axes

Knossos Palace

This room lies at the southern part of east wing in an area with many small rooms (possibly storerooms and magazines), lustral basins and light-wells. It was made into a shrine at the end of the Postpalatial period (1375-1200 B.C.). It is known as the "Shrine of the Double Axes". On a bench at the back, different ritual objects were found amongst which were a stone double axe and votive clay idols - among them the terracotta figurine of a goddess with upraised arms. Similar small shrines have been found in houses of the same period.

The House of the Chancel Screen

Knossos Palace

This house belongs to the New Palace Period (1700-1450 B.C.) and was functionally related to the Palace. In its restored part with two columns, there was a bench on which some object of worship had probably been set up. There was a paved hall in front with a double pier - and - door partition.

South East Houses

Knossos Palace

The south-east house belongs to the New Palace period (1700-1450 B.C.). It was well built and decorated with wall-paintings of lillies. It had a pier-and-door partition, a pillar room and storage rooms.

A little behind it are other houses of the Old Palace period (1900-1700 B.C.) such as the house of the "Sacrificed Oxen", named after the remains of a sacrifice found there (horns of a bull and a tripod table of offerings) and the "House of the Fallen Blocks", after the blocks that had fallen from the facade of the palace due to an earthquake.

Next to "South-East House" there are houses of the Old Palace period (1900-1700 B.C.), such as that of the "Monolithic Pillars" in front of the steps. Under the small roof is a Minoan, possibly smelting kiln.

Hall of the Double Axes

Knossos Palace

The "Hall of the Double Axes" was so named by Evans due to the double axe signs engraved on the walls of the light-well at its rear. He also thought that it was the place of residence of the King of Knossos.

The central area has openings on three sides and is therefore called a "polythyron" (system with multiple doorways). It has a slab floor and its walls were embellished with gypsum slabs and frescoes. The area between the "polythyron" and the light-well was used as a reception hall. Traces of a wooden construction were found here. Evans reconstructed a wooden throne at this spot.

According to the archaeological finds, the arrangement of the apartments on the upper floor was similar to those on the ground floor.

Queen's Megaron

Knossos Palace

The Queen's Megaron lies in the Royal Apartments next to the "Hall of the Double Axes". It is a smaller room with a similar layout and rich decoration. Evans thought that it must have belonged to the Queen. Fragments of frescoes with dolphins and dancing ladies were found here. The room is largely restored and copies of the wall paintings have been put up on the walls. At the end of the room, a low partition wall with one column created a small space. It was thought that it was the "Queen's Bathroom" since pieces of a clay "bath" were found there.

A corridor joins the "Queens Megaron" with rooms that have been interpreted as places of preparation and washing.

Magazine of the Medallion Pithoi

Knossos Palace

The magazine to the north of the Grand staircase took its name from the pithoi (large storage jars) that were found here. The jars have relief disk and rope decoration, a characteristic of the beginning of the New palace period (1700-1450 B.C.). A variety of finds show that the place had also been used as a magazine in the Old Palace period (1900-1700 B.C.).

Next door is the "Corridor of the Bays", where three small openings were used for storage. Many vases and religious artefacts were found here. The magazines were buried at the end of the New Palace period(1700-1459 B.C.).

School Room & Lapidary's Workshop

Knossos Palace

Here is the so-called "School Room", an area where, according to Evans, scribes were taught to write on clay tablets. He supposed that they kneaded the clay in the built mortar next to the bench. It is more likely, however that it was a workshop for ceramics or wall-painting.

Behind the "School Room" is the "Lapidary's Workshop", where blocks of crude or semi-worked lapis lacedaemoniae (spartan basalt) and stone tools were brought to light.

According to Evans, the main workshop lay on the upper floor from which vases and large stone amphora had fallen to the ground floor.

The magazine of the Giant Pithoi

Knossos Palace

Here the excavators found a number of very large storage jars (Pithoi) and Evans named the place the

"Magazines of the Giant Pithoi". These magazines are one of the older parts of the palace. The pithoi stand out for their size, the number of handles and the richness of their relief decoration with ropes and discs. To the right of the magazines a staircase which has been reconstructed by Evans descends to the east entrance of the Palace.

The entrance is a robust construction that gives the impression of a "bastion". From this point it would have been easy to reach an important building of the palatial period, the so-called "Royal Villa" which lies outside the main archaeological site.

The corridor of the Draught Board

Knossos Palace

The Royal Gaming Board was found here, a kind of board game made of ivory, rock crystal, Egyptian blue, silver and gold, now in Heraklion Museum.

To the right of the corridor are the "Royal Pottery

Stores", where Kamares pottery of the Old Palace period (1900-1700 B.C.) was uncovered, and to thee left, storage and workshop areas.

North Entrance & Pillar Hall

Knossos Palace

An open air narrow passage linked the Central Court with the North Entrance. It was paved and had a strong inclination towards the north. Right and left were two raised colonnades known as "Bastions".

Arthur Evans reconstructed the "Bastion" on the west side. He also placed a copy of a restored relief fresco of a bull here. The wall painting may have formed part of hunting scene.

The passage ends in a large hall with ten square pillars and two columns. The pillars and columns probably supported a large hall on the upper floor. Evans suggested that, due to its position on the seaward side, it was here that the produce of seaborne trade would have been checked when it reached the Palace. It was therefore named the "Customs House".

North Lustral Basin

Knossos Palace

This room, located beside the north entrance, resembles a cistern. Its floor is lower than the surrounding area and is reached by steps. The "Lustral Basin" was surrounded by columns and was lined with slabs of gypsum giving it a luxurious appearance. In its present form, the area has been completely reconstructed by Evans.

Areas with a similar arrangement have been found in other parts of the palace of Knossos, as well as other palaces and important Minoan buildings of the period (1700-1450 B.C.). It is not known how these places were used. However, from their construction it seems that theu would not have been filled with water, nor was there any drainage. Evans thought that they were used in purification ceremonies and therefore called these places "Lustral Basins". Evans also believed that the Palace was a sacred place. That is why, in his opinion, the "Lustral Basin"in question was used to purify visitors going into th Palace via neighbouring North Entrance.

Theatral Area

Knossos Palace

This area, sited at the north-west edge of the palace, was called the "Theatre" by Evans because its shape reminded him of later theatres. It is a platform and rows of steps that form a right angle. At the base of the stairs is the end of a narrow elevated road that crosses a paved court. Evans believed that the court was used for ceremonies watched by the standing viewers.

Excavations

Excavations first took place at Knossos in 1878 when an antiquarian businessman from Heraklion, Minos

Kalokairinos, uncovered part of the West Wing of the Palace.

In 1898, a law on archaeology drafted by the newly-founded Cretan State created the right conditions for systematic excavations that began in March 1900 under Arthur Evans, then Director of the Ashmolean Museum in Oxford. Two years later, the excavation of the Palace had almost been completed. In the years that followed, supplementary research was carried out, which came to an end in 1930-31.

After World War 2 the British School of Archeology continued the excavations with important results in the palace and the surrounding Minoan town.

The need for conservation of the Palace was obvious from the first years of excavation. The fragile materials with which it is built have proved particularly susceptible to weathering. During the first phase of their restoration attempts in 1905, Evans and his colleagues confined themselves to protecting the ruins. However, after 1925, Evans tried a radical reconstruction of the monument using concrete on large scale. Floors and whole architectural units were reconstructed. Wooden beams and wooden Minoan columns were made of reinforced concrete and rendered with paint. The wall paintings were restored and copies set up at different points.

Evans interventions produced a variety of reactions. It has been observed that the archaeological evidence is sometimes insufficient to support reconstruction. In other cases, the ancient remains are not clearly differentiated from modern intervention. The reconstructions were necessary for the protection of the monument. Moreover, they capture the interest of the visitors and help them appreciate the architecture of the Palace better. Others, nonetheless, think that, to a great extent, the reconstruction impose Evans's ideas as well as the prevailing aesthetics and ideological tendencies of his age on the visitors. But today, Evan's reconstruction of the Palace is an inextricable part of the monument and its history.

After World War 2, extensive restoration of the palace took place under the directors of Heraklion Museum, N. Platon and S. Alexiou. The works, however, were limited to conserving ancient walling, consolidating floors and protecting certain areas with roofing. During the nineties a great part of the concrete fabric of the Palace was conserved under the authority of the Directorate for the Restoration of ancient Monuments and the 23d Ephorate of Antiquities.

From 1996 onwards, the project "Conservation - consolidation - promotion of the Palace and archaeological site of Knossos" began, sponsored by the Ministry of Culture and administered by the "Funds for Administration of the Credits for Execution of Archaeological Works".

Historical Museum of Crete: Iraklion town

The history and culture of Crete, from the first centuries of the Christian era to our present time. An exceptional museum featuring a collection of extremely precious objects, a must see for every visitor to Crete. The museum is housed in a two storey neoclassical building, which was constructed in 1903 on the site of an earlier mansion

The Historical Museum of Crete presents a comprehensive view of Cretan history from early Christian times to the present day. It was founded in 1953 by the Society of Cretan Historical Studies, which had been established two years earlier. The museum is housed in a two-storey neoclassical building, which was constructed in 1903 on the site of an earlier mansion belonging to the Kalokerinos family. The second building, designed by K. Tsandirakis, was clearly influenced by morphological features of the earlier one, and was later listed as a historical monument. The new museum extension to the west constituted an attempt to combine traditional and modern architecture.

The original goal of those founding the Historical Museum of Crete was to collect and preserve valuable archaeological, ethnographic and historical material deriving from the medieval and modern periods in Cretan history. The process of enriching the collections, extending exhibition space and redefining the museum's aims has never ceased. Prolific research and publishing activity, the organisation of temporary exhibitions, educational programmes and the use of audiovisual media all form part of the modern educational role adopted by the Historical Museum of Crete over time. The same approach also includes the gradual re-organisation of the collections on display so as to appeal to a wider range of visitors, thus offering them the opportunity to understand the many facets of historical development on Crete from early Byzantine times to the present day.

Morosini Fountain: Iraklion Old Town

The "Morosini's fountain" or "Lions' fountain" that dominates the center of Eleftherios Venizelos square in Iraklion old town, is a landmark both for locals and visitors. A masterpiece of the Venetian era that would be the pride of any city in the world.

It was made in 1628 AD, under the supervision of the General Provisioner Francesco Morosini, to satisfy Candia's (Candia was the Venetian name of Crete and its capital - Iraklion - as well) needs for water. For this purpose an aqueduct was constructed to bring the water from the sacred mountain Giouhtas

The so called Lion's fountain.

One of the most known fountains of Heraklion, point of reference for its inhabitants, but also for the visitors.

Today it is one of the most beautiful monuments of the city situated at the center of the most busy square - Eleftherios Venizelos sq. - of the town

The Venetian General Provisioner of Candia (Crete and Iraklion in Venetian times) Francesco Morosini ordered and supervised its construction in 1628. He managed to bring water from the Archanes' springs to the thirsty town of Heraklion through a complicated - for that period - system of pipelines and channels.

The eight-lobe cistern, which is based on a special stand, is decorated with embossed mythological depictions and maritime figures like tritons, dolphins and various coats of arms, while the water was flowing from the mouths of four lions. At the very top of the fountain there was a supernatural statue of Poseidon that was standing out but fell probably due to an earthquake.

During the Turkish period the fountain went into a vulgar modulation with the addition of a baldachin (ciborium) around it which was later taken away.

Morosini, on the occasion of the inauguration coined a special medal with his figure from one side and the fountain on the other.

Loggia (Heraklion): Heraklion old town

The Loggia is an essential public building in every Venetian city, which was not absent even from the colonies.

For Candia (Venetian Heraklion), Loggia is considered to be one of the most elegant architectural monuments of the Venetian period, a representative sample of the palladian style. During the Venetian period, Loggia was the official meeting place of sovereigns and nobility where they discussed various topics that had to do with economic matters, commercial, and political ones. It was also used as a place where people passed their time, something like a combination of a Chamber and a Club. Today's Loggia is the fourth one, the others, that were built before that, were abandoned due to their position, or were destroyed by the time. The last Loggia was built at about 1628 by the "General Provisioner" Frangisko Morozini, known also by the homonymous fountain in the centre of the town. It is situated next to (Armeria)

and it is a building of a rectangular type with two floors, with doric type columns on the ground floor and ionic ones on the first floor. At the corners of the building there were square columns. The space between the columns, on the ground floor, had a low parapet, while in the middle it was open and served as the main entrance which was from the 25th August str., known then by the name "Ruga Maistra". At the upper part of the ground floor there was a frieze that consisted of triglyphs and metopes that depicted, in relief, various representations as the lion of St. Mark, trophies, suits of arms and others. The frieze of the upper floor, that it was never made, supported a special construction with statues.

After the fall of the city to the Turks, Loggia loses its old identity and glamour. The new conqueror did not feel the need of such a building which is now made into the seat of the high finance officer, Tefterdar and the secretary general who was a christian officer, responsible for the matters that concerned the Christians and the Turkish authorities.

The Tefterdar had also the jurisdiction over the "Armeria" (the storeroom where they used to keep their guns), now called "tzephanes". Loggia's adventure is still continuing even after the liberation from the Turks. The "Cretan State" proposed that the building could be used as an Archaeological Museum. After, though an earthquake that happened, it was better considered that the building was not safe and the idea for housing a museum was abandoned. Later in 1904 it was regarded that the building was ready to fall and people started, unfortunately without any care, to demolish the first floor.

The year after the building was granted to the Town Hall, with the "Armeria" in order to house some of its services. Ten years will go by until the first stone will be put officially for the restoration of Loggia. Maximillian Ongaro, who was also the curator of the architectural monuments of Venice, was in charge of the building work. Still though, the works were delayed. At the end of 1934 the "Armeria" is given to the Town Hall to house some of its services. After some years and the end of the 2nd World War the works for the restoration of Loggia and its connection, through an atrium, with the Armeria started afresh.

Today the first floor has been formed into a special hall for ceremonies and the weekly meetings of the Municipal Council and it has been accordingly furnished and decorated. The crowning of all these efforts was the awarding of the prize in 1987 from the International Organization "Europa Nostra" for the most successful restoration of a historical building with a modern use in the Greek area.

Koules Venetian fortress (Castello del Molo)
Iraklion Venetian port

A Venetian seaside fortress situated at the entrance of the old harbour. It was built by the Venetians, before the construction of the new Venetian fortification, in order to protect the pier and the port. It took its last shape in the years between 1523 - 1540 replacing another construction destroyed by an earthquake. It has been continuously repaired due to the violent waves of the sea that always used to cause damages to its stonework and foundation. It was built with big blocks of stone and it consisted of two floors. On the ground floor there exist 26 rooms that were used to house captains or to store food and ammunition. On the upper floor there are battlements for placing canons. The upper parts of the castle and the existing base of the minaret are Turkish changes. On the outside of the main sides of the castle, there are relief plaques that stand out with the lion of St. Mark, the symbol of Venice. During the Turkish period in the dark and humid rooms of the castle, the Turks used to torture and imprison the Cretan revolutionaries. Today, the castle is open to visitors and during the summer period it is used for various cultural activities (art exhibitions, music, theatre).

Heraklion Fortification

Iraklion

The fortified enclosure of the Venetian Chandakas of

the 15th century, which is still preserved today, is one of the most significant monuments of its kind in the whole Mediterranean basin.

Triangular in shape, with its base at the sea, the mighty enceinte has a perimeter of about 5.5 kilometres. The hallmark of the defensive layout are the bastions, linked by curtain walls decorated at many points by escutcheons and the lion of St. Mark, symbol of Venetian omnipotence. The gates in the enceinte, which served to link the town to the countryside, still stand as important architectural monuments.

To this day, the walls that withstood the Ottoman siege in the mid-17th century mark out the boundary of the old town.

Agios Titos Cathedral

Iraklion Old Town

With the recovery of Crete from Nikiforos Fokas, the

seat of the bishopric is transferred from Gortyna to Chandakas, which became the capital of the island. The new cathedral, which is the most established and largest in the city, is dedicated to the Apostle Titos. Here, amongst other relics, there are gathered the Holy Skull of the Apostle and the miraculous icon of Messopapaditissas.

When the Venetians took over Crete, they installed in the orthodox bishop the Latin archbishop, converting by that the church of St. Titos into a Latin bishop. In the middle of the 15th century, the Latin archbishop, F. Dandolo is renovating the church. Other distractions, caused by earthquakes and fire, resulted to the rebuilding of the church from the start around 1557. The church was a basilica, almost square in shape, with a dome in the middle and a bell-tower in the southwest corner.

The church from the inside was divided in three aisles with two series of columns. During the Turkish period, the church was given to Fazil Ahmet Kioprouli and it was changed into a mosque, while the bell - tower was transformed into a minaret. The big earthquake of 1856 destroyed the temple which is being, once more, rebuilt. After the exchange of populations, the Church of Crete repaired it accordingly, and in 1925 it was dedicated again to Apostle Titos. East of the church there was the building of the archdiocese.

Agios Minas Cathedral:Iraklion Old Town

The Cathedral of St. Minas:The small church of St. Minas did not meet the religious needs of the constantly growing Christian community, so the demand arose for the erection of a new cathedral. The plot for the new church used to be a garden that belonged to a Turk from whom it was bought. The architect was Athanasios Moussis and in 1862 the foundation stone of one of the most magnificent and impressive Greek churches was laid. The outbreak of the Cretan revolution of 1866 demanded the stopping of the building work which will continue in 1883 in order to be completed in 1895, when the inauguration of the exquisite temple took place. The church is of the cruciform type with a dome based on a high spandrel, while internally there are also elements of a three aisle basilica. It has two bell towers, one in the northeastern corner and the other in the southeastern one.

The right aisle is dedicated to Apostle Titos and the left one to St. Ten Martyrs of Crete. The inside of the church has gone through many changes with new additions. With plans of the architect Anastasios Orlandos the woodcut icon screen was replaced by another one made of marble, the same happened with the bishop's seat. The religious painting of the church was assigned to St. Kartakis who followed faithfully the principles and the models of the Byzantine icon painting. The hundredth anniversary from the inauguration of the Cathedral Church of St. Minas (1995) was celebrated with every solemnity that is suited in an equal occasion and more specifically to one of the most glorious and imposing Greek churches.

Saint Mark Basilica: Heraklion old town

The Basilica of Saint Mark is one of the most important Venetian buildings-monuments in Heraklion. Today it houses the city's Municipal Art Gallery. The Venetians, wishing to consolidate their dominance over their new colony (Heraklion) and to express their gratitude and love for their mother country, built a church in the city's centre dedicated to Saint Mark, patron saint of Venice. The Basilica managed to survive various earthquakes which afflicted Heraklion over the centuries with only minor repairs. During the Turkish rule it was converted into a mosque, the Defterdar Mosque, named after Defterdar Ahmet Pasha, the head of the financial department. The Ottomans demolished the bell-tower of the basilica and raised a minaret in its place, which in its turn was taken down by the residents of Heraklion after the liberation of the island in their attempt to erase the unpleasant reminders and symbols of the Turkish occupation

Agia Ekaterini church and Exhibition: Iraklion

Agia Ekaterini church and Exhibition of Byzantine Art and Ecclesiastical objects. A small sinaitic church of St. Catherine with a Basilica design, houses an exhibition with works of art from the Cretan renaissance. Among the exhibits are some of the most important icons of the Cretan School, ecclesiastical books and manuscripts, vestments, ecclesiastical vessels and relics, wall-paintings, wood-carvings and sculpture.

Agia Aikaterini of Sinai Monastery, which originally was a dependency of the Monastery of the same name on Mount Sinai, today belongs to the Metropolitan church of Agios Minas. This was an important cultural and artistic centre of Crete under Venetian occupation, until the capture of Chandax (Heraklion) by the Ottoman Turks in the 17th century (1669).

During the Venetian occupation, the Monastery housed a school, in which it is said that many important men of letters taught in the 16th century; among them were Ioannis Morezenos, Ioasaph Doreianos, Ieremias Palladas. Students of the same school were the later patriarchs Meletios Pegas, Kyrillos Loukaris, and Meletios Vlastos.

Monastery of St. Peter and St. Paul: Iraklion Old Town

It is situated approximately in the middle of the seaside wall. It was built from the first years of the venetian domination and belonged to the monastic order of Dominicans (Domenicani Predicatori). It was one of the most important and biggest Catholic monasteries of the city. The earthquake of 1508 caused a lot of damages to the temple. It consists of a long aisle which is roofed by a two slope roof and ends at a sanctuary roofed by two vaults. To the north and south wall of the temple there are windows of different types that were opened either during the Turkish period, or even earlier.

Martinego Bastion - Kazantzakis tomb: Iraklion

The bastion heart shaped in plan with an acute angle, has two "piazza bassa" and one cavalier. It defines the southeast and the highest part of the fortification. Its name is due to Gabriele Tadini Martinego (1520) who started the construction of a circular tower at the place of the later bastion. It was one of the strongest bastions (the others were that of Pantocratora and that of Vittouri) which also suffered the main attack and most of the bombardment from the Turks.

On the top of the bastion itself there was made a cavalier (which looks like a smaller bastion), whose main purpose was the better defense and control of the area around the bastion.

The grave of Nikos Kazantzakis, the famous Cretan writer, is situated on the highest point of the Venetian fortification at the Martinego cavalier. The inscription by the wooden cross reads: " I hope for nothing. I fear nothing. I am free ", a phrase taken from "The Odyssey" which Kazantzakis considered as one of his most significant works.

The playgrounds of the Academy of the local football team "Ergotelis" are located today on the main bastion and in the ditch around the bastion are the botanical gardens of the city.

Agios Georgios Gate: Iraklion Old Town

The Gate of Agios Geórgios (GR: Πύλη Αγίου Γεωργίου - Saint George also called the Gate of Maroula or Lazaretto) was one of the central gates of Chandax during the Venetian period. Today it connects Eleftherias Square with Ikarou Avenue and at the same time is used as an exhibition venue.

The gate used to lead towards the eastern provinces of the city, the Maroula suburb and the Lazaretto. Designed by Giulio Savorgnan and dedicated to St. George, the monumental city side facade featured a relief medallion of the warrior saint on horseback, set directly above the finely carved stones that formed the main portal. This monumental facade was demolished in 1917 for the opening of today's Democratias Avenue. Of the gate today, its entrance towards Ikarou Avenue is preserved, the internal domed hall and part of its climbing arcade which have been restored by the Municipality of Heraklion.

Bembo fountain: Iraklion

It was made by "capitano" Gianmatteo Bembo between 1552-1554, it dominates in today's Kornarou square, next to a later Turkish philanthropic fountain. It is decorated with coats of arms and other elements of the renaissance and of gothic type, while in the middle a big headless statue stands out of the roman period. The spring is ornated with floral and embossed elements.

Philanthropic fountain (Koubes):Kornarou square, Iraklion City

It was built in 1776 by Hadji Ibrahim aga. In order to keep it working, he dedicated almost all his property. It is unique in its kind that is still preserved today. It is of a circular type building with a "tholos" and around the walls there are semi-circular windows with rails, in front of each one of them there exist a tap with a stone basin for the water to be collected. Today it is used as a coffeehouse.

Battle of Crete Museum: Heraklion

The Museum of the Battle of Crete and National Resistance (1941-1945) was founded by the Municipality of Heraklion in May 1994.The museum's aim is to collect, preserve and exhibit relics from 1941-1945 in an appropriate manner, as well as to document and disseminate information on the people's struggle during the Battle of Crete and the German-Italian occupation.

In addition to presenting a range of material witnesses to the past, the museum aims to cultivate interest and respect for the history of Crete.

Contact details:

Doukos Beaufort and Merambellou Str.

Tel. (+30)2810 246 554

Priuli Fountain: Iraklion

The «General Provisioner» Antonio Priuli made it in 1666 and it is situated today behind the "Bodosakeio" Primary School (in the area of the Venetian Dermata Gate). He decorated it with round and square columns with Corinthian type capitals, while a triangular pediment crowns the whole construction. From both sides of the columns there are niches with their metopes elaborately decorated. In the middle of the fountain there is a Turkish inscription where there is a reference to the name of the Turkish pasha who managed to bring water again in the fountain.

Chaniali fountain: Iraklion Old Town

It is next to the external Gate of St. George, underneath the statue of Eleutherios Venizelos. Within an arched construction, which its top is decorated with floral elements, there is a plaque and the spout is within a relief decorated frame. The water was collected in a marble basin of a similar decoration.

Idomenea's fountain: Iraklion Old Town

It was built in the end of the 17th century. Today it is found behind the Historical Museum of the city. It is decorated with two columns with floral capitals, while in between them and inside an arched construction there is a marble plaque with relief decoration. The water was running from a specially made hole at the bottom of the plaque, into a marble basin.

Genitsar aga's fountain: Iraklion

It is in the Ikarou Avenue, next to the Epigraphic Collection of Heraklion Museum. Within an arched construction which, is surrounded by two big square columns, decorated with rosettes, there is a relief spout of fine workmanship. The water is gathered in a marble basin adorned by a richly decorated relief.

Sagredo Fountain: Iraklion Old Town

It was made by Giovanni Sagredo between 1602-1604, part of it has been built in the Northwest corner of today's Loggia (Town Hall) and it is decorated with a carved female statue which according to Gerola's description probably with the left hand she was holding a shield, while with the right one a kind of a big hammer for display, representing the personification of Crete.

Chania City

History of Hania Town

3000 - 2800 BC	Archaeological artifacts prove the existence of ancient Kydonia
2800 - 1150 BC	Minoan civilisation. Ancient Kydonia is one of the most powerful cities in Crete
1st millennium AD	Kydonia prevails until the 7th century AD
823 - 961 AD	Occupation by the Arabs
961 - 1252 AD	Byzantine period
1252 - 1645 AD	Occupation by the Venetians
1645 - 1897 AD	Occupation by the Turks
1898 AD	Foundation of the Cretan State. Chania is the capital of Crete

1913 AD	Unification of Crete with Greece

Hania is built on the site of the ancient city of Kydonia. This site was inhabited from Neolithic times and through all phases of the Minoan Period. The ceramics found on the hill of Kasteli, east from the port, is the earliest testimony of human presence and activity. The geographical location of the prehistoric settlement was ideal, not only because it was next to the sea, but also because it was surrounded by the rich valley of Chania. Kydonia developed into a very important center of the Minoan civilization and it was famous for its pottery workshops.

Kydonia was the first city that confronted the Roman army. Despite its strong resistance, the city was finally conquered by the Romans. The Roman General Cointos Kaikilios Metellos the Cretan, as he was called after his victory, managed to conquer Kydonia in 69 B.C, and shortly after, the whole island of Crete.

During the Roman period Kydonia was an important city. The ancient theater of the city was preserved until 1583 when it was demolished by the Venetians to use the building material for the construction of the city walls. Kydonia was destroyed in 828 AD by the Saracene pirates. During the Byzantine period Hania ceased to be an important city.

When the Venetians came they settled in Kastelli, the hill which commands the harbour, and they fortified it. They built there their cathedral, Santa Maria, as well as a palace, theatre and houses for their nobility. The city flourished as an economical and intellectual center. The fear of a Turkish invasion forced the Venetians to enclose the entire town with a wall and a moat.

A new modern city was then constructed within the city walls and significant private and public buildings were built, such as the Cathedral of Panagia (Virgin Mary), the house of the Rector and the houses of the Venetian Commanders. The public buildings were built lengthwise the central road (corso- today the street "Kanevaro") that crosses Kasteli to the east.

In 1645 the Turks occupied Hania after a two months siege. They converted old Catholic Churches into Mosques and constructed new Mosques in the city. They also founded public baths, from which only three are preserved today, as well as public water fountains, usually located next to the Mosques. Other public buildings were also constructed, such as hospitals, barracks and other military buildings, the Venetian fortress was reinforced and the urban plan was limited within its limits.

The city of Chania becomes the headquarters of the Turkish Pasha.The great 1821 national revolution shattered the relations between the Turkish and the

Greek population in Crete and bloody massacres took place in the city of Chania.

After the end of the revolution, Crete was assigned to the Regent of Egypt, Mehmet Ali, until 1841. During the Egyptian occupation, the breakwaters and the famous Egyptian lighthouse were constructed in the port of Chania.

In 1841 the 2nd Turkish period begins with the reclamation of Crete by the Turks. In 1850, the city of Chania is declared the capital of the island, because of the frequent revolutions in the region of western Crete. New public and private buildings were constructed, following the modern neoclassic styles of architecture, and the city gradually acquired a European character and was extended outside the city walls. New temples were built, such as the Cathedral temple of "Trimartyri", as well as new Municipal Departments, schools, ect.

With the liberation of Crete from the Turks, in 1897, Hania became the capital of the autonomous Cretan State. In 1913, along with the rest of Crete, it was united with the rest of the Greek State. Hania was the birth place of one of the greatest statesman of the new Hellenic Republic, Eleftherios Venizelos.

Venizelos' influence on the history of Greece was paramount, from his participation to the talks with the Ottomans that resulted to granting Crete independence in 1897, to the final union of Crete with Greece in 1913.

Cultural life

The cultural background of Chania is very rich, first of all due to the town's long history and its interaction with many diverse civilizations in the past. Furthermore the location of Crete (immediately connected to Athens; situated between Europe, Asia and Africa) as well as the cosmopolitan atmosphere that tourism creates, have generally kept the town up-to-date with modern advances in art and knowledge. Currently, there are several museums, art galleries, theatre and music groups, educational and research institutions within the city.

The Archaeological Museum located in the Old Town, houses findings from different parts of the county and from several historical and prehistorical periods of the local history (Neolithic to Roman). Within the Old Town, there is also a Naval History Museum as well as the Byzantine/Post-Byzantine Collection and a Folklore Museum. Also, the city boasts its Historical Archive (the second most important in Greece), a War Museum, the House of E. Venizelos and the Municipal Gallery.

Several theatre groups are active in Chania with the most important being the Municipal and Regional Theatre of Crete. The repertoire includes old and contemporary plays from Greek and foreign writers. The Venizelian Conservatory of Music (established 1931) is also one of the most important cultural societies in Crete. A recent attempt from the municipality to create a chamber music group named "Sinfonietta" has been successful and its performances throughout the year have enriched the cultural event calendar of the city.

During the summer period a variety of cultural events take place on a daily basis. Theatrical plays, concerts and several exhibitions from Greek and foreign artists are organized either by the municipality or by individuals. A venue which hosts many of these events is a theater located in the Firkas fortress. Also, several festivals, conferences or sport events take place in Hania especially between May and September. The Venizeleia athletics competition is one of the most noteworthy events of the year.

Hania is the base of Technical University of Crete. The studies that the university offers are related to electronic engineering, environmental engineering, production engineering, mineral resources, scienes and architecture. Other educational institutions located at the greater area of the city are the Hania branch of the Technological Educational Institute of Crete and the Mediterranean Agronomic Institute of Hania. Other research and intellectual insitutes and societies in Hania are: the National Research Foundation "Eleftherios K. Venizelos", the Mediterranean Architecture Centre (KAM), the Institute of Olive Tree and Subtropical Plants of Hania, the Philological Society "Chrisostomos", the Institute of Cretan Law and the Historical, Laographical and Archaeological Society of Crete.

Sightseeing

Hania Archaeological Museum

Hania

The museum is housed in the katholikon of the Venetian monastery of St. Francis. During the period of the Turkish occupation it was the Muslim mosque of Yussuf Pasha, while in modern times it was used as a cinema or a storehouse for military equipment. Since 1963 it has been functioning as the Archaeological Museum of the city. Apart from the permanent exhibition, the museum houses temporary exhibitions in the frame of certain local events

25 Chalidon Str., tel. +30821 90334

It contains impressive finds from the excavations of the ancient city of Kydonia, from Idramia, Aptera, Polyrinia, Kissamos, Elyros, Irtakina, Syia, Lissos, Chania, Axos, and Lappa.

Chania Lighthouse

Hania harbour

Chania lighthouse, the jewel of the city, is one of the oldest light houses, not only in Greece and the Mediterranean, but also in the world. The lighthouse (Faros GR: Φάρος) is a major attraction in the old port of Chania especially at night when it's lit up. The tower is 21m high and is built on a stone base, located at the end of the old harbour's pier opposite to the fortress of "Firkas". Visitors are not allowed to enter the tower. Chania lighthouse was first constructed by the Venetians around 1595 - 1601, and it took its final form, in the shape of a minaret, during the Egyptian Period (1831 - 1841) in around 1839. After the latest restoration, completed in 2006, it was given the formation of the Venetian period. The minaret look is still evident however.

Hania Municipal Market

Hania town

The Market, impressive for its size and shape, is built in the shape of a cross with 76 shops grouped according to their wares in the four arms of the cross. The south façade is particularly well constructed out of chiseled limestone, in the architectural style of the local tradition, developed during the Venetian period. Its construction was completed in 1913 and the formal opening was made by Eleftherios Venizelos on 4th December 1913 as part of the celebrations for the Unification of Crete to Greece.

Byzantine and Post-Byzantine Collection of Chania

Hania, old town

The wealth of archaeological material yielded by excavations conducted over many years by the 13th Ephorate of Byzantine Antiquities in the county of Chania, and also by retrieval of material and donations, forms a Collection that records, with great clarity, the history of the westernmost county in Crete from Early Christian times to the period of Turkish rule. Representative examples of this Collection are displayed in the church of San Salvatore.

San Salvatore Monastery

Hania, old town

The Franciscan monastery of San Salvatore, that houses the Byzantine and Post-Byzantine Collection of Chania, was built on the west side of the fortress of Chania, in three phases from the 15th century until the late Venetian period (middle of 17th century). The extensive restoration of the church made it possible to identify more clearly the various building phases of the monument, unify the space, and display its austere, uncluttered architectural features to good effect. The original church, which probably dates from the 15th century, was the small domed section on the east side.

Firka fortress

Hania harbour

The fortress on the northwest side of the port was constructed to protect the entrance of the port and maintains its Turkish name "Firká" (Firka=barracks). A chain from "Firka" to the lighthouse blocked the entrance to the port in case of intrusion. The fortress was the headquarters of the Army Commander of the city.

Maritime Museum of Crete

Hania, Venetian port

A two storey house, located at the old port of Hania, with a total area of 840 m2. The exhibition includes about 2,500 exhibits, such as models of ships, different kinds of naval instruments and devices, paintings, heirlooms, gleanings from the sea bottom, shells, photographs etc., which are divided in 13 units, covering chronologically all the periods.

The Venetian Shipyards (Neoria)

Hania, old port

The south complex was completed in 1599, with the construction of 17 Neoria. Today only 7 survive out of the 17. In their original form they were open on the side of the sea. The ceilings are arched, and they are connected with arched openings of the same thickness as the walls.

Rethymnon city

Réthymnon (GR: Ρέθυμνον) is the capital of the Prefecture of the same name and it is built between two other large cities of Crete. In the east is Iraklion (80 km) and to the west is Hania (60 km).

It lies along the north coast, having to the east one of the largest sand beaches in Crete (12 km) and to the west a rocky coastline that ends up to another large sand beach after 10 km.

It is the administrative, communications and commercial center of the Prefecture with approximately 25.000 inhabitants.

Today the city's main income is from tourism, many new facilities having been built in the past 20 years.

Agriculture is also notable, especially for olive oil and other Mediterranean products. It is also the base of the Philosophical School and the University Library of the University of Crete and the School of Social and Political Sciences having 8.000 students on its university campus "Galos".

Access

There is direct connection all year round from the port of Rethymnon to Piraeus.Tours to Santorini are also organized during the summer.

Rethymnon does not have an airport but the city is served by the airports of Hania and Iraklion.

Public buses can be used for travelling to Hania, Iraklion and most of the towns and villages of the Prefecture of Rethymnon.

Rethymnon Old Town

The town still maintains its old aristocratic appearance, with its buildings dating from the 16th century, arched doorways, stone staircases, Byzantine and Hellenic-Roman remains, small Venetian harbor and narrow streets.

The small port of Rethymno

I was of great strategic importance during the Venetian period. It was only able to accommodate small ships. From 1300 until today, the Venetian port has undergone numerous constructions. The 1618 wall that surrounds the port from the east is restored today with some recent interventions and additions. The original lighthouse was constructed during the Turkish period and was later replaced by another one. The building on the southeast part of the port was constructed in 1931 and functioned as a customs office. On the same location it is estimated that there was a quarantine house during the Venetian period. The vaulted spaces on the two or three-floor buildings at the port have been transformed to little and picturesque fish taverns, where visitors can enjoy the secrets of the Cretan cuisine.

The Venetian Loggia

an elegant building of the 16th century, that used to be a Venetian gentlemens's club and today houses the information office of the ministry of culture and a sales point of the archaeological museum.

Rimondi fountain

with rich decoration is situated at Platanos square, the centre of the Venetian town. It was built in 1626, by A.Rimondi, in order to provide the citizens with drinkable water.

Neratzes mosque

formerly the Holy Virgin church, was converted into a mosque by the Ottomans. Today it is used as a music conservatory. Outstanding elements of this building are the doorframe and the three domes. Next to the mosque there is the impressive minaret, built in 1890.

Kara Mousa Pasa Mosque also a venetian monastery

that was turned into mosque by the Turks. Today it is the house of the Restoration Board.

Porta Guora the entrance to the Venetian town is the only remnant of the defensive wall.

Folklore & history museum

(Vernardou 28-30. Open Monday to Friday 09.30-14.30. Closed Saturday and Sunday.) Housed in a restored Venetian building with an interior courtyard. Eight halls with collections that include textile and basket weaving, embroidery & lace, costumes, ceramics, historic photographs and maps, weapons and coins. Over 5.000 items dating from the 17th to the 20th century are displayed.

The Archaeological museum of Rethymno

(8am to 3pm, closed on Monday), just opposite the entrance of the fortress, exhibits objects from the Neolithic to the Roman period, found at the prefecture of Rethymno (mainly Eleftherna, Monastiraki and

Armeni). Clay figurines, funerary coffers, grave offerings, statues, grave steles, red-figure vases, bronze vessels, jewellery and glass vases, are some of the objects on display.

The Fortezza castle

at the top of a low hill named "Palaiokastro" dominates the town. It was built in 1590 to protect the city from the pirates raids and the Turks.

The name "Palaiokastro which means 'The old Castle" was in use even by the Venetians which demonstrates the existance of an even older castle at this place. - Probably the acropolis of the ancient town of Rithymna.

The interior of Fortezza accommodated the following basic buildings: the storeroom of the artillery, where canons and weapons were kept, the residence of the Councillors, where one of the city's two Venetian councillors lived, the residence of the Rector, which represented a luxurious, magnificent building in the central square of the fortress.

Today parts of those buildings, as well as of some others built later, can be seen. The view from up there is magnificent, especially at night.

The municipal theatre "Erofili" stands also at Fortezza's premises. It is an outdoor theatre that hosts almost all the performances during the Renaissance Festival.

The municipal gardens are ideal for those in search of shade and tranquillity.

Throughout the year various activities are organized which draw a large crowd. The Wine Festival is held there annually at the beginning of July. Another festival is held on 7-8th of November, in memory of the destruction of Arkadi Monastery.

Facilities

Rethimnon is a city that caters to the needs of the visitor.

There are a lot of places to stay ranging from luxury

hotels to rent a room, bed and breakfast apartment buildings.

Night life can range from extremely intense on the pubs and bars around the harbor and inside the old city , to relaxed on small bars right on the beach.

There is always fresh fish to be found in the tavernas around the harbor and there are many other restaurants and tavernas outside the city in equally attractive surroundings.

Shopping could also be interesting at Rethimno. There are lots of small shops with attractive merchantise from souvenirs, cards, etc to the most rare kind of sponge.

Cultural Life

Apart from enjoying the beaches, excursions into the realm of nature, good food and a drink of raki, the town of Rethymno also offers plenty of entertainment and revelry throughout the year. The most important event constitutes the Renaissance Festival, which is organised each summer since 1987, in order to revive both the Cretan and the European Renaissance. Most of the events take place in the theatre "Erofili", which is situated on the hill of the Fortress. To walk on the path, which is paved with cobblestone, uphill to the "Fortezza" on a summer evening and to live the delightful moments of a theatre, dancing or music performance is a blissful experience.

Rethymno Renaissance Festival Video

In winter the town of Rethymno lives in the rhythm of Carnival. Here, the grandest carnival on the island of Crete is organised. Apart from the great parade on Shrove Sunday, a large number of activities complete the framework of the Carnival festivities. The locals devotedly and cheerfully prepare for this season with creativity, they sacrifice their spare time and become young again while rejoicing and celebrating parties almost on a daily basis. More than 4,000 people have worked feverishly for months in order to present their masks and carriages on the great Carnival parade…The following day, on Shrove Monday people from the countryside play a leading part in the festivities. Unique traditions are revived in the villages and everybody is invited to participate in games, street performances and satires as for example "the kidnapping of the bride", the "Cadi", the "smudging of people". These performances in combination with good wine and the music of the lyre are a successful formula for a unique experience.

History

There are evidences that Rethymnon city is built on the site of ancient Rithymna that flourished during Mycenean times. In the 3rd century AD, for some unknown reason, it lost its importance, and is only mentioned as a large village. However, Rithymna retained its autonomy and independence, as is evidenced by the coins which, as a free city, it continued to mint. One of these coins is today depicted as the crest of the town with two dolphins in a circle.

During the Byzantine period the town continued to be inhabited, and parts of Roman and Byzantine mosaics have been found.

Rethymnon became a city during the Venetian occupation. The Venetians needed an intermediary port for their operations for their ships travelling from Iraklion to Hania. They also needed an administrative center, so Rethymnon became the third bigger city in Crete and an important cultural center.

The Venetians, fortified the city and called it Castel Vecchio. After that a land wall was built according to the drafts of the architect Michele Sanmicheli, which was completely destroyed in 1571 during the devastating attack of the pirate Cheireddin Barbarossa.

The 20m high tower with the sundial was demolished in 1945 In an effort to widen the exixting street.

In 1573 the construction works of the fortress of Rethymno began, which should set seal to the Venetians' final securing of their position. At this stage luxurious public buildings and private mansions were built, while the city was embellished with a central square, a Club of the Nobility (Loggia), fountains such as that of Rimondi, a large sun dial, a main road and smaller alleys, which led to the churches, the monasteries, the mansions and the simple dwelling houses according to the model of town planning in Venice.

At the same time an unparalleled stimulus was given to the intellectual development of the area.

However, in the flower of the Renaissance the Turkish invaders abruptly ended this movement, and, imposing Muslim elements, contributed to the change of the

Rethymno area into a multi-cultural community.

The Turks besieged Rethymno In September 1646

The invaders occupied the Venetian mansions, adding their own architectural elements and emphasising their presence with mosques and minarets. In the former alleys of the Venetian street network of Rethymno the buildings changed their appearance, since wooden balconies were added to the facades as extensions of the upper floors of the buildings. Thus the city achieved a different character, that of a Muslim town. During the period of Ottoman rule, Rethymnon fell into decline as did the other towns in Crete. During the difficult years of the struggle for independence, its inhabitants were actively involved and, as a result, many of its freedom – fighters were executed.

In 1897, the Russian army took Rethymnon and held it until 1909. In 1913, it became part of Greece, together with the rest of Crete.

During the German occupation, the Rethymniots took

an active part in the resistance against fascism.

In the last 25 years, Rethymno has seen a significant growth, in economy by the development of tourism and in culture by the operation of the university.

Sightseeing

Rethymnon Old Port: Rethymnon town

Rethymnon old port was of great strategic importance during the Venetian period. It was only able to accommodate small ships. From 1300 until today, the Venetian port has undergone numerous constructions. The 1618 wall that surrounds the port from the east is restored today with some recent interventions and additions. The original lighthouse was constructed during the Turkish period and was later replaced by another one. The building on the southeast part of the port was constructed in 1931 and functioned as a customs office. On the same location it is estimated that there was a quarantine house during the Venetian period. The vaulted spaces on the two or three-floor buildings at the port have been transformed to little and picturesque fish taverns, where visitors can enjoy the secrets of the Cretan cuisine.

Rethymnon Fortezza: Rethymnon town

The Fortezza castle, at the top of a low hill named "Palaiokastro" dominates the town. It was built in 1590 to protect the city from the pirates raids and the Turks.

The name "Palaiokastro which means 'The old Castle' was in use even by the Venetians which demonstrates the existance of an even older castle at this place. - Probably the acropolis of the ancient town of Rithymna.

The interior of Fortezza accommodated the following basic buildings: the storeroom of the artillery, where canons and weapons were kept, the residence of the Councilors, where one of the city's two Venetian councilors lived, the residence of the Rector, which represented a luxurious, magnificent building in the central square of the fortress.

Today parts of those buildings, as well as of some others built later, can be seen. The view from up there is magnificent, especially at night.

The municipal theatre "Erofili" stands also at Fortezza's premises. It is an outdoor theatre that hosts almost all the performances during the Renaissance Festival.

Contemporary Art Museum of Crete: Rethymnon Old Town

The Contemporary Art Museum of Crete was founded in 1992 as Municipal Gallery 'L. Kanakakis'. It is housed in a Venetian building at the old city of Rethymno, below the Fortezza fortress and the Archaeological Museum. It houses a permanent exhibition of the work of Lefteris Kanakakis (oil paintings, sketches and aquarelles), thus representing all the stages of his achievements, as well as works of contemporary Greek artists, which cover a broad spectrum of modern Greek art as it has been accomplished from 1950 until today.

Address: 5, Heimaras Str. 741 00 Rethymno

Tel: +30 28310 52530

Website :www.rca.gr

Rethymno Archaeological Museum: Rethymnon Old Town

It is located just opposite the entrance of the fortress (Fortezza). It exhibits objects from the Neolithic to the Roman period, found at the prefecture of Rethymno (mainly Eleftherna, Monastiraki and Armeni). Clay figurines, funerary coffers, grave offerings, statues, grave steles, red-figure vases, bronze vessels, jewellery and glass vases, are some of the objects on display.

Historical and Folklore Museum of Rethymno: Rethymnon old town

The Historical and Folklore Museum of Rethymno is located next to the Neratze Mosque. It is an institution of public benefit, founded in 1973 by the President of the Historical and Folklore Institution, Christoforos Stavroulakis, and Fali Vogiatzaki. The museum is housed in a restored Venetian building with an interior courtyard. The building is a wonderful piece of urban residence of the last phase of the Venetian occupation of Crete, built in the renaissance style by traditional craftsmen.

Neratze Mosque: Rethymnon old town

During Venetian occupation the mosque Neratzes, which today is used as a conservatory, was the Augustinian church of the Holy Virgin. In 1657 the Turks transformed it into the mosque 'Gazi Housein' or 'Neratze', and in 1890 they added a large minaret with two galleries, which was built from the famous stones from the village of Alfa. The chapel of the Holy Virgin, situated at its west side and dedicated to the Body of Christ, was also transformed into a seminary.

Outstanding elements of this building are the doorframe and the three domes.

Rimondi Fountain: Rethymnon Old Town

A. Rimondi, the Rector of the city, built the famous Rimondi Fountain, which is situated at present day Platanos Square, formerly the centre of Venetian city life, in 1626. The water runs from three spouts in the shape of a lion's head into three sinks. Three small, fluted columns, ornamented with Corinthian capitals are "standing" on the sinks. Above the capitals an entablature can be observed, the middle part of which displays four projections in the shape of the leaves of the acanthus exactly above the columns. Furthermore in this section the words LIBERALITATIS and FONTES are inscribed.

Rethymnon Loggia: Rethymnon Old Town

Loggia has been built during the 16th century and was designed by the famous architect Michel Snamicheli.

Loggia was an eminent building of the city centre and has been a meeting point for the nobles to discuss political and economical issues. The building is very well preserved; it is square and has arches on its three sides (besides its west side). The consoles of its eaves are spectacular. During the Turkish occupation the loggia became a mosque and a minaret was constructed, which was later demolished in 1930. The past 40 decades the building of Loggia hosted the archaeological museum of the city, which has now moved to a building next to Fortezza. Today loggia hosts a market of archaeological art copies.

Saint Francis Church: Rethymnon Old Town

The church of Saint Francis is one of the most important monuments of Rethymno. It was the main temple of the Monastery of the Franciscan Order. The architecture of the building - a single aisle Basilica type with wooden roof - and its ornaments are very interesting. Next to the east side of the temple two deserted chapels are preserved. Its Corinthian style main doorway is impressive, with capitals of composite order. During recent excavations around the church valuable archeological findings have been discovered, including two tombs of Venetian nobles.

During the Turkish occupation the temple was turned into an "Imaret" (a shelter for the poor).

It was also used as a cultural center until 1996. It was recently renovated to accommodate the Byzantine and Post-Byzantine Collection of the Prefecture of Rethymno.

Kara Mousha Pasha Mosque: Rethymnon Old Town
The Mosque took its name from the Turkish commander of the marine operations to conquer Rethymno, in 1646. During the Venetian Period, the Mosque became a monastery dedicated to St. Barbara. West from the central building, there is the deserted minaret of the mosque. The fountain of the Mosque is

attached to the roofed entrance of the Mosque's garden, where believers washed before entering the Mosque and provided the area with fresh spring water.

Square of Mikrasiaton: Rethymnon Old Town

The square of Mikrasiaton (GR: Πλατεία Μικρασιατών) formerly the 1st primary school square, in Rethymnon town, covers an area of 7,500 square meters, right at the heart of the city's historical center. It is surrounded by valuable monuments and beautiful buildings, mainly used as cultural centers.

There, visitors have the opportunity to rest in a peaceful environment and at the same time visit the various monuments and cultural centers located in the area.

Guora Gate (Porta Guora): Rethymnon Old Town

The Guora Gate (Porta Guora or Grand Gate)) is the main entrance of the Venetian city walls that protected the city of Rethymno. The gate was built in the years of

Rector Rettore Jocopo Guoro (1566-1568). Part of the gate is preserved at the beginning of the street "Ethnikis Antistaseos". It is 2,60 m. wide, built with carved stones with skew acnes, creating a semicircular arc on the top.

According to traveler J. Gerola, the initial shape of the gate was formed by stepped cornice and pediment where a relief the lion of St. Marcos (the Venetian emblem) existed. Today the relief is preserved in two pieces and is stored at Loggia's courtyard.

Marine Life Museum of Rethymnon: Rethymnon Old Town

The Museum of Submarine Life is situated at Arapatzoglou street, at the center of Rethymno's old city. It was founded by the "Moshaki" family, in memory of their lost child, who drowned in the sea. The largest part of the exhibits are made up of shells, while a few vertebrates, sponges and fish are also on display.

Agios Nikolaos city

Agios Nikolaos, capital of the Prefecture of Lasithi, is one of the most highly developed tourist towns in Greece.

It lies along the west of the Mirabello bay. The main road axis of the island passes right outside the city limits , connecting it with Iraklion (66 km) to the west,Sitia to the east (70 km) and Ierapetra to the south (36 km).

Agios Nikolaos is the administrative, communications, cultural and commercial center of the Prefecture, with approximately 8500 inhabitants.

The climate in the area is mild with extremely low humidity. It is an ideal place to relax and recover one's energy.

Access

There is frequent bus service from Iraklion. There are boat connections all year round from the port of Agios Nikolaos to Piraeus. During the summer there are also connections with the islands of Cyclades and with the islands of Kassos, Karpathos, Kos. Tours to Santorini are also organized during the summer.

Agios Nikolaos does not have an airport but the city is served by the airports of Iraklion (Nikos Kazantzakis) and Sitia.

Attractions

The sea in Agios Nikolaos is superb and the surrounding area of the city is noted for its sandy beaches and beautiful bays - Kitroplateia, Ammos beach, EOT beach and Ammoudi are within walking distance from the city center.

The landmark of the city is definitely the small lake, known as "Voulismeni" that is located in the center of the city, at the foot of the cliffs. Its shape is circular with a diameter of 137m.

According to the mythology, the goddess Athena used to take her bath in this lake. The depth of the lake is 64 m and was connected to the sea only recently, with a canal opened at 1870.

It is an especially picturesque site with many open-air cafes and restaurants along the bank.

Small boats leave the harbor to visit the Venetian fortress of Spinaloga, near Elounda .

Every summer the Municipality of Agios Nikolaos organizes cultural events, music and dance events, theatrical performances, exhibitions, shows. Also, during the Naval week, artistical swimming, water skiing, wind-surfing contests are organized.

Agios Nikolaos also possesses the second finest Archaeological Museum in Crete, where splendid archaeological findings from throughout the Prefecture of Lasithi are exhibited.

History

In the site where the town is built today, used to be the ancient "Lato pros Kamares", which was the harbor of "Lato", an important and powerful city located near the village of Kritsa.

In the Roman and the first Byzantine period it also served as a harbor.

During the Venetian occupation, the Venetians built the fortress Mirabello(meaning beautiful view), in the site where the Prefecture building stands today. Nothing of the fortress is saved today, but it gave its name to the Prefecture and to the bay, that is called Mirabello.

When the Venetians built another port in the area of Elouda in the northwest, named "Porto di San Nicolo", the importance of the harbor of Agios Nikolaos lessened.

The city is named after the small Byzantine church of Agios Nikolaos, located on the peninsula. The church has fine frescoes from the 8th, 10th and 11th century.

Facilities

Agios Nikolaos has numerous and high-quality tourist accommodation of all types and class. Some of the oldest hotels are located in Eleftheria square, but there are many new fine hotels not only in the town, but all along the coast. There are also many cafes, restaurants, bars and shops.

Other Sights

Phaistos

Palace and Archaeological Site

The archaeological site, the palace, the findings - The Festos Disc. According to mythology, Phaistos (or Festos) was the seat of king Radamanthis, brother of king Minos. It was also the city that gave birth to the great wise man and soothsayer Epimenidis, one of the seven wise men of the ancient world.Excavations by archaeologists have unearthed ruins of the Neolithic times (3.000 B.C.).

Phaistos (GR: Φαιστός - also spelled : Phaestos, Phaestus, Faistos, Festus and Festos) was one of the most important centres of Minoan civilization, and the most wealthy and powerful city in southern Crete. It was inhabited from the Neolithic period until the foundation and development of the Minoan palaces in the 15th century B.C.

The Minoan city covered a considerable area around the palatial centre. After the destruction of the palace in the 15th century, the city continued to be inhabited in the Mycenaean and Geometric periods, that is, until the 8th century B.C.

The exact location of the Palace of Phaistos was first determined in the middle of the 19th century by the British admiral Spratt, while the archaeological investigation of the palace started in 1884 by the Italians F. Halbherr and A. Taramelli. After the declaration of the independent Cretan State in 1898, excavations were carried out by F. Halbherr and L. Pernier in 1900-1904 and later, in 1950-1971, by Doro

Levi, under the auspices of the Italian Archaeological School at Athens.

Although many inscriptions were found by the archaeologists, they are all in Linear A code which is still undeciphered, and all we know about the site, even its name are based to the ancient writers and findings from Knossos.

According to mythology, Phaistos was the seat of king Radamanthis, brother of king Minos. It was also the city that gave birth to the great wise man and soothsayer Epimenidis, one of the seven wise men of the ancient world.

Excavations by archaeologists have unearthed ruins of the Neolithic times (3.000 B.C.).

During the Minoan times, Phaistos was a very important city-state. Its dominion, at its peak, stretched from cape Lithinon to cape Psychion (Today cape Melissa at Agios Pavlos, South Rethymnon) and included the Paximadia islands. The city participated to the Trojan war and later became one of the most important cities-states of the Dorian period.

Phaistos continued to flourish during Archaic, Classical and Hellenistic times. It was destroyed by the Gortynians during the 3rd century B.C. In spite of that, Phaistos continued to exist during the Roman period. Phaistos had two ports, Matala and Kommos.

The most important monuments of the site are:
The Palaces (old and new). They are built of ashlar blocks and spread on different terraces. To the central, peristyle court are opened the royal quarters, the storerooms, a lustral basin, and workshops. The monumental propylon and the large staircases faciliate access to the many terraces.

Minoan and later town. Sections of the town have been located at the sites called Chalara and Aghia Photeini, SE and NE of the palace, respectively.

Venetian church of St. George of Phalandra. It lies to the west of the palace, on the left of the road that leads to the archaeological site of Aghia Triada and Matala.

Gortyn Ancient town

Messara, Iraklion South

Located in the valley of Messara, Gortys or Gortyn (GR: Γόρτυς or Γόρτυνα) is a must visit for all visitors to Crete. It was inhabited during Bronze Age times, but its rise to glory came almost a millennium after the downfall of the 'Minoans'. Gortyn was a prosperous city from around the middle of the 5th century BC through to the early 9th century AD, when it was finally destroyed by the Saracens (824AD), never to be

Gortyn is located at the Messara Valley, near the village of Agioi Deka, on the 46th km of the main road from Iraklion to Tibaki that traverses the island from north to the south. Gortyn is crossed by the river Lithaios, today called Mitropolianos, that dominates the valley of Messara.

The significance of the great ancient city of Gortyn is recognized and recorded in its rich mythological and religious tradition. Great gods, like Zeus, Europe and Demeter, but also semi gods, heroes and kings like Minos, Gortys, Rhadamanthys, as well as Iasion and the Minotaur play a leading role in its myths. Gortyn is also associated with the major figures of Christianity; the Apostles Paul and Titus, and the Holy Ten Martyrs.

Gortyn was one of the oldest and strongest cities in Crete during the prehistoric and historic period. The population of ancient Gortyn is believed to be 300.000 people. The Gortynians occupied Phaistos during the 3rd century B.C. During the Roman period reached the peak of its glory and it was the capital of Crete. Gortyn was the first city of Crete to accept Christianity, and maintained its glory until 828 A.D. when it was occupied and destroyed by the Saracens. Since then it was never inhabited again.

The most important monuments of the ancient Gortyn are the ruins of the acropolis and the Odeum. The odeum of the ancient city was the place where parts of the great Law Code of Gortyn was discovered. The Gortyn Law was inscribed on stones. Four series of inscribed stones are preserved today, which constitute relics of great importance for the study of the epigraphy and Law of the time. The inscription is in a Dorian dialect and it was written at the end of the 6th century B.C.

At the organized main archaeological site, visitors can see the Roman Odeum and the Great Inscription with the Law Code of Gortyn, the early Byzantine church of Saint Titus, and the Antiquarium next to the modern refreshment hall. Scholars and any other interested person can also visit the other major excavated monuments, providing they contact the Archaeological Service in advance and are accompanied by a warden.

The magnificent ruins of the great ancient city of Gortyn, including the Acropolis and the cemeteries, cover an area of 4 square kilometers in the middle of the Messara plain. The rectangle formed by the ruins is 2 kms long on each side. The northern side is bordered by the hills of Agios Ioannis, the Armi and the hill of Prophitis Ilias. The southern side reaches the fields south of the village of Mitropoli. To the west it extends to the western boundary of the fields belonging to the Agricultural School of Mesara, while to the east lies the village of Agioi Deka. The site is crossed by the modern roads leading from Agioi Deka to Mires, from Agioi Deka to Vagionia, and from Mitropoli to Lentas.

Besides, through the area flows the Mitropolianos River, which according to one theory is the ancient;

river Lethaios, a tributary of Geropotamos (possibly the ancient Malonites).

Gortyn is the largest archaeological site on Crete in terms of land area, and one of the largest in Greece. Foreign travellers, impressed by its ruins as early as six centuries ago, refer to the great number of statues, inscriptions, columns and other architectural fragments (up to 1500 in total).

Malia Minoan Palace

Archaeological site in Malia, Iraklion

The Palace of Malia, which covered an area of 7,500 sq.m. , was the third- largest of the Minoan Palaces and is considered the most "provincial" from the architectural point of view. The first Palace was built in 1900 BC and destroyed in 1700 BC when a new Palace was built. Following the fate of the other palaces in

Crete it was also destroyed in 1450 BC. and the present ruins are mainly those of the new

The Minoan Palace and the archaeological site of Malia are located 3 km East of the town of Malia. From the architectural point of view the Palace of Malia, is the third- largest of the Minoan Palaces and is considered the most "provincial" of them.

It covered an area of 7,500 sq.m. and according to tradition the third son of Zeus and Europa, Sarpedon, brother of the legendary king Minos, ruled here.

The Palace had two floors and its entrance is from the western paved Court, through a procession passage. It is a building with a central court, loggia, theatre, sanctuaries, Royal quarters, workshops and magazines. North of the western court is the hypostyle crypt, discovered recently, and protected from the weather conditions by a modern roof. The large underground room, whose ceiling was supported by columns, is considered as a council chamber for the political deliberations of the local lords, separated from the dwelling quarters and the official buildings. Its a forebear of the classical Greek Pritaneion, which had a similar function

History

The site was inhabited in the Neolithic and early Minoan period (6000- 2000 BC), but very little trace remain. The first Palace was built in 1900 BC and destroyed in 1700 BC when a new Palace was built. Following the fate of the other palaces in Crete it was also destroyed in 1450 BC. and the present ruins are mainly those of the new palace.

The excavations at Malia were begun in 1915 by J. Chatzidakis and were continued by the French Archaeological School. The Palace, houses in the town and the cemetery at Chryssolakos have already been excavated. The finds are exhibited in the Museum of

Herakleion, and some in the Museum of Aghios Nikolaos.

The most important monuments of the site are:
At the south west part of the central court is located a round table, with little cavities around the edge and a bigger at the center, standing on a base. This table is believed to be a kind of kernos of the classic Greece. In the cavities the Minoans put the seeds, offering to the god, so they wished to have a fruitful crop. This explanation seems more probable as this custom still exists in Crete.

At the east side of the central court, with a pillared portico, was the palace's eastern entrance near which there ware the rooms of the royal treasury. On the same side was a raw of Magazines, narrow cells leading off a communal corridor and occupied by pithoi (jars) standing on bases, with an arrangement for gathering liquids (channels and vases for oil and wine.)

About 500 m north of the palace was the necropolis, a royal burial enclosure, certainly belonging to the lords of Malia, surrounded on all four sides by leveled areas and perhaps by porticoes. Here was found the famous Bee pendant which is now on display at the Iraklion Museum. This pendant is in the shape of two bees, or wasps, storing away a drop of honey in a comb.

The ancient cemetery is located at a place named Chryssolakkos a name that means the "pit of gold" because of the precious objects that the farmers used to find there.

At the entrance of the archaeological site, there is the little two-room museum. The museum has a few minor finds and photographs since the important finds from Malia are at the museum of Heraklion. The most interesting exhibit, in the museum, is a scale model, recreating the palace complex in its glory days.

Diktaian Cave (Dikteon Antron)

Psychro, Lassithi Plateau

The cave of Psychro is one of the most important cult places of Minoan Crete. The excavators and several scholars identify the cave as the famous "Diktaian Cave", where Zeus was born and brought up with the aid of Amaltheia and the Kouretes, and which is connected with myths as this of the seer Epimenides who "slept" here, or the coupling of Zeus with Europa.

The cave of Psychro (Diktaion Antron or Diktaian Cave) is one of the most important cult places of Minoan Crete.

The use of caves as cult places was one of the basic characteristics of the religious beliefs of the ancient Cretans.

Cult practice probably begins in the Early Minoan period (2800-2300 B.C.) - although in the antechamber are preserved traces of an even earlier occupation -

but the most important finds date from the Middle Minoan period (1800 B.C.) and later, as it was used for many centuries, until the Geometric (8th century B.C.) and the Orientalising-Archaic period (7th-6th century B.C.).

The finds prove that it was visited as late as the Roman period. Pilgrims dedicated many offerings, such as figurines of humans, gods, animals, double axes etc.

The excavators and several scholars identify the cave as the famous "Diktaian Cave", where Zeus was born and brought up with the aid of Amaltheia and the Kouretes, and which is connected with myths as this of the seer Epimenides who "slept" here, or the coupling of Zeus with Europa.

In the last decades of the previous century, inhabitants of the area found ancient items inside the cave; this fact led in 1886, the archaeologists Joseph Chatzidakis and F. Halbherr to the site, where they conducted an excavation, but not on a large scale.

The cave was also investigated by A. Evans in 1897, by J. Demargne, and by G. Hogarth in 1899, but systematic excavation has not taken place yet.

The finds uncovered during legal and illegal excavations were almost all published in 1961 by J. Boardman.

The numerous offerings to the cave are now exhibited in the Herakleion Museum and the Ashmolean Museum in Oxford.

At 1,025 m. a.s.l., a steep path leads up to a plateau in front of the narrow entrance to the cave.

On the right side is an antechamber (42 x 19 m.) with a rectangular altar, 1m. high, built of field stones; this area yielded Neolithic potsherds, Early Minoan burials (2800-2200 B.C.), and offerings of the Middle Minoan period (2200-1550 B.C.).

In the northern part of the antechamber, at a lower level, a chamber is formed, which included an irregular enclosure with patches of roughly paved floor, forming a sort of a temenos.

The large hall (84 x 38 m.) has an inclined floor and a small chamber opening to the left end; one of its niches is called the "liknon" of Zeus.

A larger chamber (25 x 12 m.) formed on the right side is divided into two parts: one has a small pool, and the other a very impressive stalactite, known as "the mantle of Zeus".

Inside the main chamber had been deposited many offerings, mostly bronze figurines and sheets (1, 2), daggers, arrowheads, and double axes.

Agia Triada Arch. Site

Archaeological Site in Messara, S-W Iraklion

The "Royal Villa" at Ayia Triada which is situated very close to Phaistos, was built in about 1550 BC. i.e. just before the new palace at Phaistos, and was destroyed by fire in l450 BC, like all other important Minoan centres. It succeeded the first palace at Phaistos as the economic and administrative centre of the regions depriving the new palace there of this role, and appears to have had connections with Knossos

Four kilometers west from Phaistos are the ruins of the Royal Villa, the Small Minoan Palace at Agia Triada. The site is named after the village of Agia Triada that is located next to it and was inhabited untill 1.897, when the Turks destroyed it. The Minoan name of the site is unknown .

At the site are the Minoan town, the palace and the tombs, excavated by Halbherr with L. Banti in 1902 and onwards. La Rosa resumed the excavation after 1976.

History

Remains of a settlement and graves prove that the site was inhabited as early as the 3rd millennium B.C. In

2600-1700 B.C., the time of the heyday of the first (old) palace at Phaistos, only small building were erected in the area of the Royal Villa. The villa was built in ca. 1600 B.C. and destroyed sometime in the 15th century. An imposing "megaron" of the "Mycenaean" type was erected on its ruins (14th-11th centuries B.C.) and an extensive settlement with a portico ("agora" or market-place) developed to the north of the villa.

In the Geometric period (8th century B.C.) the site was a cult place, while in the Hellenistic period (4th-1st century B.C.) a small sanctuary was founded, dedicated to Zeus Velchanos. The single-aisled church of St. George was built in the period of the Venetian occupation (14th century A.D.).

Aghia Triada was first investigated in 1902, in the course of excavations at the neighbouring site of Phaistos. Systematic excavations were begun in 1903 and completed in 1914. Work was resumed recently in the area to the north of the Mycenaean settlement, by the Italian Archaeological School at Athens (directed by Vnicenzo La Rosa).

The central part of the Villa is protected under a shed. The rest of the monuments have been cleared and consolidated.

Monuments
The most important monuments of the site are:

The Royal Villa. It consists of two wings and, although it was smaller than the palaces of Knossos and Phaistos, it presents all the typical features of palatial architecture: halls with polythyra (pier-and-door partitions) and a light-well, shrines, magazines, repositories, workshops, staircases, porticoes, courtyards, terraces, balconies and paved streets.

The settlement and "Agora". They lie to the NE of the villa and belong to the Mycenaean period. Eight spacious rooms are opened behind the portico of the

Agora (market-place) while to the west of it are the remains of a Mycenaean settlement.

The cemetery of Aghia Triada. It includes two Early Minoan (3000-2300 B.C.) tholos tombs with complexes of funerary rooms, and chamber tombs of the Late Minoan period (14th century B.C.). Burials were placed in clay larnakes (sarcophagi). A similar larnax, made of limestone, the famous painted sarcophagus of Aghia Triada, was also found at this cemetery.

The "Megaron" of the "Mycenaean" type, built over the storerooms of the Royal Villa, is contemporary with the portico. Church of St. George Galatas. The Byzantine church, decorated with splendid wall-paintings, lies in the courtyard of the Minoan villa.

Findings

Some of the most important findings of the Minoan period were excavated in Agia Triada and are currently on display at the Archaeological museum of Iraklion.

These include three engraved clay vessels of exemplary artistic value and the famous sarcophagus the only stone sarcophagus ever to have been found in Crete

Arkadi monastery

Rethymno

The Monastery of Arkádi (GR:Αρκάδι) built during the last Venetian period, it consists of a large set of fortress-like buildings. The main building included the cells, the warehouses where the agricultural products were treated and stored, the stables. In a word, it was a well-equipped little fortress where people could find refuge in times of trouble. There is an impressive church, with two naves

The Monastery of Arkádi (GR:Αρκάδι) constitutes a landmark of architecture and civilisation considering the magnificent façade of the church, the highly developed spiritual tradition as well as the flourishing development of fine arts. However, the holocaust, which took place in 1866, gave the monastery an eminent place in history, elevating it to an eternal symbol of freedom and heroism, which is acknowledged the world over.

The Monastery of Arkadi lies on a low plateau, 23 kilometres from the town of Rethymno. Built during the last Venetian period, it consists of a large set of fortress-like buildings. The main building included the cells, the warehouses where the agricultural products were treated and stored, the stables. In a word, it was a well-equipped little fortress where people could find refuge in times of trouble.

The elaborate central entrance was restored just four years after the 1866 explosion. It leads to the interior court, through a vaulted passage. In the middle of the court, stands the impressive church, with its two naves dedicated to Saint Constantine and Saint Helen, and to Our Lord.

Completed in 1587, its façade clearly shows the different currents in the development of Cretan art during the 16th and 17th centuries.

In the south-west corner of the church, one can still see a section of the burnt iconostasis that survived the 1866 holocaust.

The church is surrounded by a large and roomy precinct and the vaulted passages with their row of arches have retained their grandeur. The cells on the three sides of the court and the communal rooms on the north side are impressively austere.

The history of the monastery goes back to Byzantine times, when a monk, possibly named Arkadios, founded the monastery which in turn was named after him.

Already in the 16th century the monastery played an important role in the cultural life of Crete. There were many copyist monks, a rich library and a school.

The Turkish invasion reduced its cultural activities for a while, but the Arkadi Monastery was able to recover promptly and received a unique privilege among Greek monasteries: the Turks allowed the ringing of its bells.

The monastery proved to be not only a remarkable cultural centre, but also played an all-important role in the fight against the Turks: when the Turkish Army (15,000 men) surrounded the monastery in November 1866, 300 fighting men and 600 hundred women and children had taken refuge in it.

When the walls came tumbling down and the Turks began the massacre, one of the rebels, Kostis Giamboudakis, blew up the powder magazine and the sky-high explosion reduced the monastery to a pile of rubble. This heroic feat is considered one of the greatest in Cretan history and has turned the Arkadi Monastery into one of Europe's Monuments to Freedom. There's a museum in the monastery with many impressive relics of the 1866 Holocaust and some beautiful icons. Many efforts have been made for the restoration of the monastery in the last years.